Welcome to Storytime!

The Art of Story Program Planning

Library Use Only

By Rob Reid

UpstartBooks

Madison, Wisconsin

Dedicated to Betty Freij

"As you ascend the angels
remove your weights
beginning with those on your legs
so you can dance and
dance and
dance."

—R. R.

Published by UpstartBooks
4810 Forest Run Road
Madison, Wisconsin 53704
1-800-448-4887

Table of Contents

Introduction

Planning for story programs is more than grabbing a handful of random picture books off the library shelves and sharing a couple of Mother Goose nursery rhymes. There is an art to developing a cohesive succession of picture books and "in-between activities"—finger-plays, musical and movement activities, poems, creative dramatics, and art projects. Taking the time to develop a carefully constructed story program experience makes for a highly participative, extra-special literary activity that not only will become the talk of the town, but will also help children become lifelong readers and library users.

If time has gotten away from you and you can only manage to grab a few random stories off the shelves to read, there is still value in the activity—you are sharing literature time with children who live in a day and age of electronic entertainment overload. There are several ready-to-go story program lesson plans on the market to help with these scenarios. But if you'd like to take your story programs to another level, not only for your audience, but also for yourself, consider the process described in this book.

When I first began conducting public library story programs, I did indeed pull a few random picture books off the shelf and read one after another to groups of children. Many lost interest at various points during the 30-minute program. After receiving a suggestion from a more experienced librarian that I should insert some fingerplays between the books, I did so . . . with pretty much the same results.

That's when I decided I needed to spice up my programs. I wanted to have memorable experiences with these children. What helped me achieve that goal over the next three decades were my efforts to:

- Be choosier about the picture books I share

- Look for picture books with breezy texts that lend themselves to audience participation (e.g., sound effects, some type of movement, or a call-and-response moment)

- Be more expressive, not only while reading picture books, but also during my interactions with children at the beginning of the programs, between picture book readings, and at the end of the programs

- Add more music to the programs

- Add more movement activities (these last two rules meant much more when I finally gave myself permission to be noisy in the library)

- Create my own original material (There is a lot of pride that comes from making up even a simple, four-line fingerplay verse.)

Welcome to Storytime! is divided into three parts. **Part One** covers *preparation*, which explains the process of creating effective story program lesson plans—i.e., selecting the books and creating engaging "in-between activities."

Part Two focuses on *presentation* and features eight original story program lesson plans and an outline of the thought process behind their creation. Each plan contains four or five picture books and three or four in-between activities. The plans create an approximately 30-minute program. Typical audiences for these programs tend to be preschoolers (usually in a public library setting) or primary-grade children (usually in a public library or elementary school library setting). The lesson plans in this book work well for both age ranges.

Part Two presents the final lesson plan first, followed by a detailed explanation of "How I Got There." This section will cover the initial inspiration for the program theme, the "Scavenger Hunt" (search techniques for locating the best picture books to fit the program), "The Choices" and "Back-up Books Selection" (picture books that were ultimately selected), "Locating and Developing the In-Between Activities," and finally, "Program Presentation" with detailed storytelling tips that make suggestions for putting it all together.

When you read through Part Two, keep in mind that the books and activities selected for these programs are done so to create a high energy, interactive, and fairly humorous storytime. But within this fast-paced program, there should also be a quieter, slower segment—perhaps the sharing of a gentle story, reading a reflective poem, or moving to a laid-back activity. This allows both the storyteller and the children in the audience to catch their collective breath and ramp up the energy towards a fun ending.

Part Three features a collection of some of my favorite original fingerplays, poems, songs, musical activities, and movement activities. Many of these have appeared in various issues of *LibrarySparks* magazine and some UpstartBooks titles, and this is the first time they have been gathered in one publication. Please use and adapt them freely. It is my hope that they will ultimately help you create your own material.

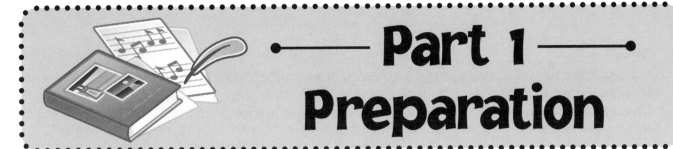

Part 1
Preparation

Where to Start

Q: Where to start when planning a storytime program?

A: Begin with just a kernel of an idea.

<u>That idea may be to feature a **particular book.**</u>

When I found the picture book *Press Here* by Hervé Tullet (Chronicle Books, 2011), I knew I had to feature it in a story program. *Press Here* is an inventive book that speaks directly to readers. It asks them to press the "buttons" painted in the illustrations, blow on the pages, and shake the book.

The lesson plan I built around *Press Here* could have gone in a few directions. I had some young children exclaim, "It's magic!" *Hmm,* I thought. *Perhaps a magic theme would fit.* But *Press Here* is also a highly interactive book. Perhaps a theme called "Move It" could be developed. Then there was the Library of Congress, which gave the book the subject heading, "Toy and Moveable Books." Perhaps the whole story program could showcase similar toy books, such as pop-up and lift-the-flap books.

In the end, it was the wide eyes and smiles on the children's faces that *Press Here* inspired that led to the "Smile" story program found in Part Two of this book.

<u>That kernel of an idea may be a **song you've heard.**</u>

For example, after hearing "Nocturnal" by Billy Jonas from his recording *What Kind of Cat Are You?* (Bang a Bucket Music, 2002), I thought of doing a lesson plan featuring animals that are active while we're sleeping. It was easy to pull up a list of nocturnal animals from the Internet and go searching for picture books and activities featuring raccoons, flying squirrels, deer, mice, crickets, and owls. Further examples of song-inspired themes can be found in the next section, Thoughts on Themes.

<u>That idea may come from the **calendar.**</u>

Perhaps a monster program around Halloween, a program about rain in April, or a summer-related program about picnics or vacations will work for your audiences.

<u>That idea may come from a passing **comment.**</u>

A young patron might say, "I like cowboys." A few days later, you're planning an American western lesson plan that not only features cowboys, but also cowgirls, coyotes, snakes, and horses.

No matter where the idea originates, start small and build upon it. The notion of building a program around an inspirational initial idea is further explored in Part Two.

Thoughts on Themes

There are many storytellers who don't use themes in their programs, and they do fine. As I mentioned earlier, I like to use themes because they give me focus when planning. However, I sometimes get caught up in the "theme trap," in which I pick a theme first and then look for books and activities to fill the lesson plan. Occasionally, this may lead to limited results and sub-par material, simply because the material fits the theme. Again, it can be much easier—and fun—to find a picture book or song that you like and can't wait to share, and then build a theme around that book.

If you find two books that you like and can't wait to share, look for a common thread between them and build a theme around that thread. For example, when *Click, Clack, Moo: Cows That Type* by Doreen Cronin (Atheneum, 2000) came out, I had just found the book *Old Cricket* by Lisa Wheeler (Atheneum, 2006). Instead of using the first book in a farm- or cow-themed program, and an insect theme for the second book, the alliterative nature of both texts led to the development of a program titled "Clickety-Clackety, Creaky-Squeaky Stories." The program showcased books with these alliterative features, such as *Double Trouble in Walla Walla* by Andrew Clements (Milbrook Press, 1997) and *The Squeaky, Creaky Bed* by Pat Thomas (Random House, 2003). There were also several tongue twisters and other wordplay built into the program. My search process in this case was simply to paw through the picture book section. It turned out to be a fun, simple, and rewarding search.

Also, again, listen to the music in your mind and in the world around you. If there's a particular tune going through your head that you've recently heard on the radio, consider using it as the basis of a story program theme. In the past, I developed a food/cooking theme after hearing the folk song, "All around the Kitchen" from the recording *Family Dance* by Dan Zanes (Festival Five, 2001). Other songs that inspired entire story programs include "Baby, You Can Drive My Car," a car-based theme inspired by a line from "Drive My Car" by the Beatles (Rubber Soul, EMI, 1965); "Heat Wave," a theme about all things hot, inspired by "(My Love Is Like a) Heat Wave" by Martha and the Vandellas (Live Wire, Motown, 1972); "Hot Fun in the Summertime," a similar hot-based theme centered the summer season, inspired by a song by Sly and the Family Stone (Greatest Hits, Epic, 1970); "I'd Like to Be under the Sea," an ocean theme, inspired by a lyric from "Octopus's Garden" by the Beatles (Abbey Road, Apple, 1969); and "The Weather Outside Is Frightful," a winter theme inspired by the Christmas song "Let It Snow."

It's important not to limit your theme. If you do decide to search for material after you've chosen a theme and your search results in several so-so picture book choices, try broadening your theme to allow for more results. For example, if a search for a story program about elephants brings up only one or two exciting elephant books, expand the theme to include other large mammals—in this case, large *gray* animals. With hippos, rhinos, and whales added to the mix, there may be several more strong titles from which you can now choose. I once was searching for books for a penguin storytime session, and the lesson plan was a book or two away from being a dynamic program. I broadened the search to include other black and white things: zebras, panda bears, skunks, Dalmatians, and even soccer, with the black and white soccer balls. The initial penguin theme morphed into a fun story program called "What's Black and White?" The program can now have books added that feature red things (fire engines, apples, the Little Red Hen), and morph once more into "What's Black and White and Red All Over?"

Building a story program around a letter of the alphabet can also be fun. Find characters and objects that begin with a particular letter. For example, an "O" theme I created came about from a desire to showcase the Olivia books by Ian Falconer. Again, pawing through the picture book collection was an easy way to come up with the rest of the titles for the program. There were a lot of choices: stories and activities about owls, opossums, the ocean, otters, Old MacDonald, *Joseph Had a Little Overcoat* by Simms Taback (Viking, 1999), *Officer Buckle and Gloria* by Peggy Rathmann (Putnam, 1995)—even books by Kevin O'Malley and Helen Oxenbury.

Playful Themes

Often in my workshops for teachers and librarians I tell them, "If you're looking for ideas about teddy bear and bunny rabbit programs, you've come to the wrong place." I didn't really mean it—it's just a set-up line to inspire creativity. Personally, I've had fun doing teddy bear and bunny rabbit programs, and once, after delivering this set-up line over and over, I worked on the two themes and created a combined "Teddy Bears and Bunny Rabbits" program. But while there is obviously nothing wrong with bears and bunnies, it is important to remember that storytellers have a wealth of non-traditional, playful themes waiting to escape their imaginations. The following is a list of some of my favorite original themes that worked well for me over the years. Use them to inspire your own playful themes.

- Alien Space School (You wouldn't believe how many books there are about aliens going to school. Who knew?)
- Altered Endings and Twisted Tales: Stories and Activities that Feature Fractured Fairytales
- B Is for Bulldozer: Stories and Activities about Construction Equipment
- Baby, You Can Drive My Car: Stories and Activities about Automobiles, Motorcycles, Trucks, and Buses
- Bad Hair Day: When Hair Doesn't Behave
- Big and Bad: Stories and Activities about the Villains in Children's Stories
- Big and Gray: Stories and Activities about Elephants, Hippos, and Rhinos
- Boo Ha-Ha: Not-So-Scary Scary Stories
- Catching Some Zzzzzz's: Stories and Activities about the Last Letter of the Alphabet
- Down and Dirty: Stories and Activities about Life Underground and Being Dirty and Messy

- Eeee-Yuu! Gross-out Stories and Activities (These stories featured worms, garbage, slugs, etc.)
- Give Me a B! Give Me Another B! (You'd be surprised by how many books, songs, and nursery rhymes have two words in the title that both start with the letter B. There is *Baby Beluga* by Raffi [Crown Publishers, 1992], *Baby Beebee Bird* by Diane Redfield Massie [HarperCollins, 2000], *Bootsie Barker Bites* by Barbara Bottner [Putnam, 1992], Little Boy Blue, and more.)
- Heat Wave: Stories and Activities about Summer and Hot Weather
- I'd Like to Be Under the Sea: Stories and Activities about the Beach and the Ocean
- I'm Telling! Stories and Activities about Naughty Kids and Animals
- Itsy-Bitsy, Teeny-Tiny Tales: Stories and Activities Featuring Small Characters
- I've Got the Blues: Stories and Activities Featuring Emotions
- Meow and Squeak: Stories and Activities about both Cats and Mice

- Mirror, Mirror on the Wall: Folktales and Fairy Tales
- Morning, Noon, and Night: Stories and Activities Starting with Waking Up, Going through the Day, and Ending at Bedtime
- Mouth Sounds: Stories and Activities Featuring Sound Effects
- Nocturnal: Stories and Activities about Creatures that Are Awake While We're Sleeping

- Oh No! Stories and Activities that Feature the Letter "O"
- Picky Eaters: Stories and Activities about Foods that Kids Don't Like
- School Talent Show: Stories and Activities that Feature the Arts in School
- Shake It All About: Stories and Activities about Dance and Movement
- Super Baby: Stories and Activities about Babies Who Don't Act Like Babies
- Super Kids: Stories and Activities about Super Heroes and Everyday Heroes
- Sweet Tooth: Stories and Activities that Feature Sweets (and also Healthy Food)
- Tales from the Treetops: Stories and Activities about Trees
- Talk like a Pirate Day: Stories and Activities about Pirates and Buried Treasure
- Three (The number three is a common number in many folktales.)
- Vitamin C: Stories and Activities featuring the Letter C
- What Stinks? Stories and Activities about Bad Odor
- Yes, No, Maybe So: Stories and Activities about Behavior

"Quick and Dirty" Themes

After all this talk about well thought-out themes, I know some of you are thinking, "OK, Reid. Enough already! Not everyone has the time to create programs like this!" You're right, and I must confess that I still do some "quick and dirty" story programs and call them "Rob's Favorites" or "Fun Stories for Kids." I'll sometimes rifle through the new book cart and call the program "Something New." However, I often don't get the same satisfaction that I get from doing the more time-consuming, creative themes. It's a matter of prioritizing your time. Still, for those times when you're caught short, check out the idea for a creative version of "Quick and Dirty Themes" at the conclusion of Part Two.

Finding the Best Picture Books

The next step in the process is to locate the best picture books to use in your program. If you start your search on the library online catalogue, write down words that relate to the theme and plug them in for both word and subject searches. For example, if creating a "B Is for Bulldozer" theme, think of relatable terms: "construction," "construction equipment," "trucks," "bulldozers," "cranes," and "diggers." Use word searches to find those few titles that might not have been assigned a corresponding subject heading by the Library of Congress.

While it may be tempting to grab the first four or five books you find, I recommend taking the time to locate about a dozen books. This gives you a larger field from which to choose. Read each one and consider the following:

- Does the text flow? Are there particular words or phrases that come to life when read aloud?
- How long is the text? Every once in awhile, a well-written lengthy text can enchant a group of young children, but for the most part, short, concise texts work best in a typical story program.

- Is there potential for audience participation while reading the text? Are there any phrases that suggest natural movements or sound effects for the audience to make while you read?
- Does the text have a pattern? Repetitive phrases are great for audience participation. The kids can say them along with the storyteller after hearing them read aloud a few times.
- Can the illustrations be clearly seen by most of the audience? Of course, there will be those children who say they can't see the pictures no matter how you display them. If the text is wonderful, but the pictures are hard to show, go ahead and use the book. The children can look at the pictures after the program.
- Is there some kind of connection with one book that you've found with any others you're considering? In other words, when one book is finished, is there a natural segue to another book?
- Does reading the book bring to mind any song or rhyme you can use in connection with the book?
- Can you see any potential for sharing the book as a flannel story? With puppets? With props?

From this field of books, choose the four or five that best suit your program. Select another two or three titles as backups in case you find you still have time to fill, or if one of the primary books you chose is just not working with a particular crowd.

Choosing the Order of the Picture Books

Once the books are chosen, it's time to decide on the order. One general rule that librarians have followed for ages is to begin the program with the longest, least participative book and work your way down to the shortest book with the most amount of participation. I believe this still holds up as a good method, but sometimes it's best to veer from the rule if the natural transition from one book to another is more important to the cohesiveness of the entire program. I often tweak the standard rule by starting the program with something short and sweet to grab everyone's attention, and placing the longest book second in the order. For the lesson plan "Yawn" found in Part Two of this book, the first picture book is *Don't Let the Pigeon Stay Up Late!* by Mo Willems (Hyperion, 2006). It's fairly short, very silly, and features a character that talks directly to the audience. It starts the program off with a bang.

Locating In-Between Activities

After choosing the books' order, it's time to start looking for in-between activities that go in-between picture book readings. They help keep the children's attention and add nice variety to the overall program. In-between activities are often:

- Fingerplays
- Movement activities (that use the whole body, not just the fingers and hands)
- Songs
- Musical activities (songs with movement)
- Poetry/nursery rhymes and wordplay (jokes, riddles, tongue-twisters, raps)
- Creative dramatics/reader's theater
- Puppetry
- Crafts

Personally, I usually choose something musical, something with movement, and some form of poetry or wordplay. I do so because I feel these are my strengths as a storyteller, and I particularly enjoy sharing them with children. Early in my career, I felt I had to use every form of in-between activity. My predecessor spent half of her story programs doing crafts, and that's what patrons had come to expect from a story program. I personally don't enjoy craft activities as much as music, movement, and wordplay. It took awhile, but eventually I gave myself permission not to include them. The same thing happened with puppets. I tried using them, but I knew I could craft a stronger storytime program without them.

If you enjoy using puppets and sharing craft activities, by all means, utilize them. If not, figure out what you do like. If you enjoy sharing clapping songs, then clap away! If you don't feel confident sharing music, perhaps you'd be more comfortable with a chant, poem, or movement activity. You might even decide to cut down on the amount of in-between activities in a program. If so, then add another book to read. Play to your strengths. Use whatever format gets you excited.

A Core Collection of Resources

The following are my favorite resources to locate songs and musical activities for storytime programming:

- *Children's Jukebox*, 2nd edition (ALA Editions, 2007). This is my own reference work that locates recorded songs by subject.

- Camp song websites, such as The Ultimate Camp Resource (www.ultimatecampresource.com) and Scoutorama (www.scoutorama.com). Similar sites can be found by searching "Camp songs" in most Internet search engines. Not all of the songs found on these sites are ideal for young kids, but many do work well in children's story programs. Screen for appropriateness.

- The Kididdles website (www.kididdles.com) contains a mix of camp songs and copyrighted children's songs.

- The Wee Sing series by Pamela Beall and Susan Nipp offers recordings with booklets containing lyrics and directions to many traditional children's songs. A complete list of the Wee Sing recordings can be found on their website (www.weesing.com).

The following are my favorite resources for locating fingerplays and movement activities:

- 1,000 Fingerplays and Action Rhymes by Barbara Scott (Neal-Schuman, 2010). This is a comprehensive source of traditional and original fingerplays and action rhymes.

- Any Mother Goose collection.

- Gayle's Preschool Rainbow (www.preschoolrainbow.com).

- YouTube (www.youtube.com). Search for fingerplays and you can view several storytellers performing dozens of interesting fingerplays.

- Again, the Wee Sing recording booklets offer lyrics and directions to several spoken fingerplays and poems.

Once the activities have been chosen, place them within the lesson plan between the picture books. There doesn't need to be an activity between each and every picture book, but don't read more than two picture books in a row before having a corresponding activity. Wherever possible, position the activities with the most movement near the end of the lesson plan, similar to the order structure of the picture books. Many times, the order of the picture books changes in order to accommodate the activities.

Creating Your Own Fingerplays and Song Lyrics

There are times when it's hard to find that one special fingerplay or song to use in the story program. When that happens, sit back, close your eyes, think for a few minutes, open your eyes, and start writing lines on a piece of paper.

For this particular book, I created about a dozen new activities for the eight original lesson plans in Part Two. Some are adaptations of popular rhymes and songs. Others were created from scratch. Each lesson plan goes into detail on the creative process for the in-between activities, and many aspects of the process apply to the original and adapted activities provided in Part Three. Review them, use them in your own story programs, and perhaps use them as models to help create your own works.

When you are ready to begin, start with these most basic steps for creating a new fingerplay or children's song lyric:

1. Write four lines of verse.

2. Make the last word of the second line rhyme with the last word of the fourth rhyme.

3. Repeat the process as needed.

Voila—there's your fingerplay or song verse!

Okay, it does take a fair amount of reflection, and a bit of trial and error. What actually goes into those four lines of verse? As you ponder this question, jot down words that relate to your program theme or to a specific picture book. Pick one or two words that rhyme, position them at the end of the second and fourth line, and see if you can construct coherent sentences. Write and re-write them to make them flow. For inspiration, read and re-read nursery rhymes and observe how they are constructed. If the rhymes don't work well, substitute words until you find two that do work. This is where a rhyming dictionary comes in handy. It's not uncommon for me to fill one or two pages of a legal pad with crossed-out verses before completing the final copy of a four-verse rhyme.

For a case study, take a look at "But Mostly I Love You" in the "All You Need Is Love" lesson plan in Part Two. A short movement activity was needed between two of the picture books: *And I Love You* by Ruth Krauss (Scholastic, 2010) and *I Love You Through and Through* by Bernadette Rossetti-Shustak (Scholastic, 2005). I began by jotting down objects and concepts that dealt with love. I then came up with the notion of having the children pointing up, pointing down, and twirling all around as the verse was read to them. There was a fair amount of rewriting to keep the lines simple for a young audience. The following verse turned out to be the next-to-final draft:

"I love, I love the sky so blue,

I love the earth down below,

I love this world so very much,

My love will grow and grow."

I constantly read my verses out loud, rewriting anything that doesn't flow. This particular version was clunky and the last sentence didn't fit the other three verses. I got stuck on finding a rhyme for the word "below." The problem was solved when I switched the first and second lines. It was then easy to come up with a rhyme for the phrase "sky so blue." That turned out to be "I love you." After writing and scribbling, scribbling and writing, this is how the final version turned out:

"I love, I love the earth below,

I love the sky so blue,

I love this world so very much,

But mostly, I love you."

The new last verse also worked well with the movement directions. For the last line, the children can point to someone else or simply straight ahead. Yes, some may think the verse is pedestrian and overly simple. However, *it works in the context of a children's story program!* When it was done, I was almost as excited about writing this four-line verse as I get when I write a whole book. I ran around to family, friends, and neighbors saying, "Hey! Listen to this!"

Many storytellers will write new verses for traditional rhymes and songs. This is a wonderful way to create new material for story programs. For example, if you need an activity to go between two picture books featuring penguins, mull over popular nursery rhymes and children's songs and think of lyrics that match your theme. Sometimes, you only need to alter a few words or phrases from the original rhyme or song. Consider the traditional song "The Ants Go Marching." Swap ants for penguins and tweak the other words in the verse. "The penguins all march in a line/ Hurrah, hurrah."

Some of my favorite adaptations over the years included changing the words of "Head, Shoulders, Knees, and Toes" to "Dogs and Cats and Guinea Pigs" for a pet theme; "The More We Get Together" transformed into "The More We Brush Our Teeth" for a dental theme (both of these adaptations can be found in Part Three); and rewriting "The Itsy Bitsy Spider" for "The Eensy Weensy Robot" activity found in the "Toyland" lesson plan in Part Two. I have made variations of "Going on a Bear Hunt" many times. I've led kids on elephant hunts, duck hunts, raccoon hunts, and more. I frequently make new versions of "Old MacDonald." One version is "Old McDonald Had an O," in which we make sounds and movements of things that begin with the letter "O" such as octopuses, onions, ogres, and operas. Another favorite is "Old MacDonald Had a Jungle," where we make monkey and parrot noises instead of cow and pig sounds. These, too, are located in Part Three.

Another great source for adaptation are traditional songs, rhymes, and fingerplays that are based on counting backwards or forwards. Think of "This Old Man" or "Five Little Monkeys Jumping on a Bed," which starts out with five monkeys and works its way to no monkeys. Consider writing a fingerplay that follows this model. "Three Little Aliens," found in Part Three, uses this format.

Look over the following roster to see if any of the rhymes and songs listed there inspire you to develop your own set of lyrics. Work with your theme. Look at each rhyme and song on the roster and think to yourself, "Is there something here I can use?" Recite the original words of the rhymes and songs aloud. This may lead you to change first one line, and then another. If you are unfamiliar with any of the titles on the roster, it is easy to find the lyrics and/or sound clips for most of them on the Internet, or on the children's music recordings indexed in *Children's Jukebox*. All rhymes and songs on the roster are in the public domain.

A Roster of Popular Rhymes and Children's Songs to Inspire New "In-Between Activities"

- The Alphabet Song
- The Ants Go Marching
- Apples and Bananas

- Baa Baa Black Sheep
- Bingo
- Do Your Ears Hang Low?
- The Farmer in the Dell
- Five Little Monkeys Jumping on the Bed
- Five Little Monkeys Swinging in a Tree
- Going on a Bear Hunt
- The Grand Old Duke of York
- Head, Shoulders, Knees, and Toes
- Here We Go Loop de Loo
- Here We Go 'Round the Mulberry Bush
- The Hokey Pokey
- I Had a Rooster
- I Know an Old Lady Who Swallowed a Fly
- If You're Happy and You Know It
- I'm a Little Teapot
- I've Been Working on the Railroad
- The Itsy-Bitsy Spider
- Jingle Bells
- Kookaburra
- London Bridge
- Mary Had a Little Lamb
- The More We Get Together
- My Bonnie Lies over the Ocean
- Old MacDonald
- Over in the Meadow
- Pop Goes the Weasel
- Ring around the Rosie
- Rock-a-Bye Baby
- Row, Row, Row Your Boat
- She'll Be Comin' Round the Mountain
- Shoo Fly
- Skip to My Lou
- Ten in the Bed
- Three Blind Mice
- Twinkle, Twinkle, Little Star
- The Wheels on the Bus
- Where is Thumpkin?
- Yankee Doodle

Final Tips for a Successful Program

Practice

Once your lesson plan is in order, do a quick rehearsal in a quiet place where you won't be disturbed. Read and recite all the books and activities out loud. Try to feel the flow of the lesson plan. You may find that you need to make changes to the lesson plan during rehearsal. For example, based on reading a book aloud, you may decide to swap it for one of the back-up picture books that sounds better to your ear. Or perhaps you'll re-arrange the entire lesson plan order. Practice the fingerplays and other activities a few times each. You don't have to memorize each one, but practice enough to be able to perform them well without stumbling. One trick to avoid having to memorize all of the activities is to write the words or lyrics on a large sheet of paper and post it on the wall above and behind the audience. You can look over their heads and recite the words as you share the activity with them.

During rehearsal, practice holding the picture books, taking care to be aware of where your audience will be seated. Pay attention to height and determine if the children will be able to see the pictures. The storyteller is usually seated above the audience, so remember to hold the book to your side and tip the book downward. Too many storytellers tip the book upward to see the text better, but the children are not seated on the ceiling. By reading the book a few times during rehearsal, you'll be able to hold the book out to your side and have a good grasp of the words as you look at them from the more audience-friendly angle. Try to avoid stopping and starting, stopping and starting, just so you can show the pictures—the more continuous the story, the better it will be understood.

The practice time you put in before your storytime program may seem like a lot of extra work, but committing even 15 minutes to rehearsal will help take the final program presentation to another level of excellence.

Adults in the Audience

Rehearsal is over and you're ready for the kids. In public libraries, there may also be adult family members in the audience. Some library programs are aimed at combined child and adult audiences, such as family storytimes, lapsit program for infants, and toddler programs. Consider the idea of having adults sitting in preschool storytimes. When I first started conducting preschool programs, I was told by my supervisor, "No matter what, don't let the parents in." She found them distracting.

I didn't. For the most part, the adults in my programs were interested in what their child was doing. They were becoming more knowledgeable about the picture books in the collection. They were learning the words to a new fingerplay or song. If you are not comfortable having adults in the program, if you feel you are too self-conscious or you find the grownups disruptive, be sure to let them know what your policy is ahead of time.

If you do choose to invite adults to the program, you will find there are other advantages to their presence. For instance, if you have discipline problems with rambunctious kids, adults can provide assistance so you can continue with the program. During the program, adults are also likely to note the books you're using, as well as the in-between activities. Many of them will continue sharing these stories and activities at home, thereby encouraging their children to develop into lifelong readers and library users. Finally, adults who attend your storytime sessions will know what's going on with your programming and other programming in the library—and they will spread the word to their friends and other members of the community, which may even include local politicians and others who hold the budget's purse strings. You will have new advocates letting others know that library programs are vital to the families of the community.

A Few Words about Discipline: Adults and Children

As I have made clear, I like adults in attendance at my storytime programs. At times though, they distract me more than a restless child does. Usually when this happens, it is because a few adults use the time as an opportunity to sit near each other and chat—while I'm conducting a program! In these cases, I try to catch them after the program and tell them I enjoy their presence in the program area, but their talking distracts me. Or I might catch their eye during the program and raise my finger to my lips to shush them. Many times, I'll wait until we're doing an activity and announce, "I need *everyone* in the room to do this with me!" I try to be diplomatic, but clear at the same time.

When a child is being disruptive, I double my focus on the majority of the children who are well-behaved and paying attention. I can handle the disruptive child mostly by ignoring her, or quickly asking her to sit-still-because-there-are-more-fun-things-coming-up—and *boom!* We're off and running to the next book or activity, with the child's attention refocused.

If the kids say they can't see the pictures, which I can usually count on, I let them have another look and then inform them that they can look at the book again at the end of the program. For the occasional child who is very disruptive, you need to discuss the problem with the parent or childcare provider after the program. Ask the guardian to work with you on coming up with a solution. The parents may have to sit in during the program with the child on their laps, or even keep the child from attending the program for a few months until the child has matured a bit and is ready to return and behave.

I try to head off most discipline problems by having a lively, entertaining program, but sometimes, there are days when I have to stop the program entirely to get everyone settled down again. Don't hesitate to try this if things seem to be getting out of hand.

A Few Words about Burnout

When I was a practicing children's librarian, I conducted hundreds and hundreds of story programs over the course of a decade and a half. Many librarians have told me that they never suffered from programming burnout, but there was a time in my career when every so often, I felt like I had hit a brick wall, no matter how much I enjoyed my job and working with children. It was sometimes difficult to muster up enthusiasm to do that next story program. I worked hard at recognizing when that was happening, and identifying why. I talked to other librarians to see what they do in these situations. I looked at my schedule. I looked at my work habits. Ultimately, what helped me the most was to *take a break*, and *change my work routine.*

Taking Program Breaks

You have to balance the public demand for story programs with your energy to create and conduct them. As a public children's librarian, I found it very helpful to change the library's program schedule from weekly programs year-round to taking off the entire months of May, August, and December. In May, our staff was already busy enough, concentrating on getting the summer program ready. In December, the public was busy with the holiday season and demand for the library programs was lower than usual.

August was not as easy a choice; we had many parents with children out of school who were looking for something to do, and grandparents with visiting grandchildren who wanted activities. Still, taking August off after a busy summer program schedule was vital for the staff to recharge their batteries and to get ready for the school year.

When I was a consultant for a library system, I met with a burned-out children's librarian from a small, nearby community. Her director demanded that she conduct story programs all 52 weeks of the year. The director felt that was the public's expectation, and the library should meet it. The librarian lost her energy and enthusiasm. She felt her programs were suffering. I pled her case to the director, explaining that quality was more important than quantity, and the library as a whole would do better to take those program breaks. The director finally relented and a year later, the children's librarian reported that taking the breaks made all the difference in the world. She also said that the public understood.

Changing Your Work Routine

Changing your routine is basically what this book is about. For me, it was the realization that grabbing storytime books off the shelf at the last minute, sharing the same in-between activities over and over, and getting into a rut was wearing me down. My new routine for preparing story programs included coming up with unusual themes, making the search for books into a scavenger hunt, and creating new in-between activities. These steps increased the fun, as well as my enthusiasm and desire to get back into this personal and public aspect of my job: the programs.

Today, I teach college students—future librarians and teachers—the joys of sharing literature with children. I conduct volunteer story programs in my community. I also travel to libraries and schools around the country to share books and activities with children. When I start feeling burned out, I still take those invaluable breaks or mix up the routine.

The Program Area

Some librarians are forced to conduct story programs between bookshelves because there is nowhere else to go. Others hold story programs out in the open. Sometimes the furniture must be moved every time a program is held. There are libraries that have enclosed program rooms with ample space and built-in, tiered seating.

The ideal scenario is some sort of established space where there is plenty of room for both the story program leader and the audience—not only when sitting, but also when standing and moving about. There should be room for a chair and a small table to hold books and props. If you use puppets and felt boards, you will need room for those, too.

If your program is held out in the open on the library floor, you will no doubt have to "train" the other patrons to expect that each week, for this 30-minute period, the joint will be jumping!

Opening and Closing the Program

I always have music playing as the children enter the program. There are hundreds of wonderful children's recordings on the market, and it's fun to have subtle songs playing that relate to the program theme for that day. For instance, if conducting a program about the environment, have Raffi singing "Evergreen, Everblue" from the recording Evergreen, Everblue (Shoreline, 1990) in the background. If you feel comfortable doing it, make small talk with early arrivals—the children who are already seated and waiting for others. The informal chat tends not only to relax the children a bit, it also gets them looking forward to the program.

Once everyone is seated, you can launch right into the opening book or activity, or perhaps give a small introductory greeting such as, "Welcome to storytime. I'm excited to be here and I hope you are, too. I have some fun books and songs and activities to share with you. Sometimes I'll need you to be really quiet so that everyone can hear me. Other times, I may ask you to help me tell a story by making some noise. I'll let you know when. Let's get started!"

You may want to open with the same song or opening chant each program; *Children's Jukebox* has a list of nearly fifty "hello" songs. A few of the more simple, easy-to-learn songs include "A New Way to Say Hello" from the recording *Big Jeff* by Big Jeff (Big Jeff Music, 2000), "Hello" from the recording *Peanut Butter, Tarzan, and Roosters* by Miss Jackie (Miss Jackie, 1981), and "Hello Everybody" from the recording *Hello Everybody* by Rachel Buchman (A Gentle Wind, 1986).

When the program comes to a close, thank the children for coming. Tell them you hope they find some wonderful books to take home. You may use a poem, song, or saying to share at the end of each program. I always end with my poem "Wave Goodbye." The lyrics and motions can be found in Part Three.

Consider making a half-page handout that includes the titles of the books read in the program, and the words to the activities. Give these to the parents, grandparents, and babysitters who didn't sit in the program.

It is my hope that the suggestions I've provided in Part One will help you elevate not only the quality of your story programs, but also your excitement about presenting them. In Part Two, you'll see my thought process about sharing each theme, each book, and each activity with children.

Part 2 — Programs

A-A-A-Choo! Stories and Activities about Being Sick

Final Lesson Plan

1. Opening Picture Book: *Sneezy Louise* by Irene Breznak. Illustrated by Janet Pedersen. Random House, 2009.

2. Song: "The Sneezing Song" by Jim Gill from *Jim Gill Sings the Sneezing Song and Other Contagious Tunes* (Jim Gill, 1993).

3. Picture Book: *A Sick Day for Amos McGee* by Philip C. Stead. Illustrated by Erin E. Stead. Roaring Brook Press, 2010.

4. Poem: "Turning Into" by Shel Silverstein from *Everything On It*. HarperCollins, 2011.

5. Picture Book: *Bear Feels Sick* by Karma Wilson. Illustrated by Jane Chapman. Margaret K. McElderry Books, 2007.

6. Movement Activity: "I Don't Feel Good" by Rob Reid.

7. Picture Book with Felt Characters: *Felicity Floo Visits the Zoo* by E. S. Redmond. Candlewick Press, 2009.

8. Song: "Mary Had a Little Cold," traditional. New words by Rob Reid.

9. Closing Picture Book: *Pigs Make Me Sneeze* by Mo Willems. Hyperion, 2009.

How I Got There

Initial Inspiration

This theme came about after I read *Pigs Make Me Sneeze* by Mo Willems around the same time I discovered *A Sick Day for Amos McGee* by Philip Stead. The illness connection was an obvious thematic choice, and I got to work finding other material to fill out the program.

The Scavenger Hunt

I selected the other picture books through the library catalog by searching the subject "Illness – Juvenile Fiction." A word search was also used with the term "Flu." A few titles were found with these terms. The catalog records of these titles revealed that they were assigned similar headings: "Sneezing – Juvenile Fiction," "Food Allergies – Juvenile Fiction," "Influenza – Juvenile Fiction," "Diseases – Juvenile Fiction," and "Cold (Disease) – Juvenile Fiction." These additional headings yielded more than a dozen potential picture books.

The Choices

- *Bear Feels Sick* by Karma Wilson has nice large illustrations and a breezy text to read aloud.
- *Felicity Floo Visits the Zoo* is a funny story with a small gross-out feature. The many animals and handprints found in the book can be used to turn this into a felt story.

- *Pigs Make Me Sneeze* by Mo Willems. This man's books are hilarious, and *Pigs Make Me Sneeze* has great audience participation possibilities.
- *A Sick Day for Amos McGee* by Philip C. Stead. This Caldecott Award-winner for best illustrations has a comforting and logical storyline. It's a nice contrast to the silliness found in the other choices.
- *Sneezy Louise* by Irene Breznak is a cumulative pattern story with audience participation opportunities.

Back-up Books Selection

- *Farm Flu* by Teresa Bateman. Illustrated by Nadine Bernard Westcott. Albert Whitman, 2001. Cartoon-style illustrations work well with the absurd aspects of the book.
- *Llama Llama Home with Mama* by Anna Dewdney. Viking, 2011. This entry in the bestselling Llama Llama series has nice large illustrations and a simple verse text.
- *Sneeze, Big Bear, Sneeze* by Maureen Wright. Illustrated by Will Hillenbrand. Marshall Cavendish, 2011. Like Wilson's *Bear Feels Sick*, this book features large animals and nature illustrations with a flowing text. I went back and forth between *Sneeze, Big Bear, Sneeze* and *Bear Feels Sick*, and opted to go with the latter since there were already two picture books that dealt with sneezing.

Choosing the Order of the Picture Books

Sneezy Louise made a good opener. It has the longest text of the books and will immediately involve children with the repetitive refrain, "Geez, Louise! COVER YOUR MOUTH, PLEASE!" as well as the chance to make sneezing noises. *A Sick Day for Amos McGee* and *Bear Feels Sick* are nice, gentle stories, so they went second and third to provide an opportunity for a mellow period early in the program. Placing these titles here also made the whole program seem more cohesive. *Felicity Floo Visits the Zoo* went fourth. The felt characters add a nice variety for the audience to focus on, especially this far along in the program. *Pigs Make Me Sneeze* ended up the program because it is a quick read, and the sneezing connection between *Pigs Make Me Sneeze* and *Sneezy Louise* make a nice bookend to the program. Also, it gave the kids a chance to make the loud sneezing sounds one more time.

Locating and Creating the In-Between Activities

The first thing I did when searching for in-between activities was to check *Children's Jukebox*. My eyes zoomed right in on Jim Gill's song, "The Sneezing Song." Many Jim Gill songs are highly participative, so it was worth a listen, and this one goes particularly well with *Sneezy Louise*.

Shel Silverstein's poem "Sick" from *Where the Sidewalk Ends* (HarperCollins, 1974) has been a popular choice in story programs over the years. When his posthumous collection of poems, *Everything On It*, was published, a quick search found a nice substitute for "Sick" in the form of the poem, "Turning Into."

While musing about the sneezing opportunities that the opening and closing picture books would provide for a young audience, the song "Mary Had a Little Lamb" popped into my head. I thought about changing the title to "Mary Had a Little Sneeze," and then decided "Mary Had a Little Cold" sounded better. (One doesn't have a sneeze; one sneezes. One has a cold.) The lyrics came easily because I had sneezing on my mind, and the finished song worked well right before the final picture book, *Pigs Make Me Sneeze*.

Still, the program needed one more activity. "My Name Is Joe" came up in a search through the camp song sites. The piece directs kids to move their body parts in all directions. I sat down and wrote a list of things that happen when we're sick, and then matched these things with body parts. This is how the call-and-response movement activity "I Don't Feel Good" was written. I placed it between the quiet book, *Bear Feels Sick*, and the visually appealing *Felicity Floo Visits the Zoo*.

Program Presentation

Opening Picture Book: *Sneezy Louise*

Louise's eyes are itchy, her throat is wheezy, and her nose is "sneezy." When her mother places a bowl of oatmeal in front of her, Louise sneezes and oatmeal flies everywhere. At school, Louise's sneezes send papers scattering. Her sneezes also trip up dancers at ballet school, upset a bowl of peas at dinnertime, and distress her family and pet dog at bedtime. She catches one final sneeze with a tissue before falling asleep, knowing that "tomorrow would be an easier day."

Storytelling Tips: The children will instinctively join in by making sneezing noises and chanting the refrain, "Geez, Louise! COVER YOUR MOUTH, PLEASE!" They will know when to sneeze with the set-up line, "She knew that she was going to . . ."

Song: "The Sneezing Song"

After each verse, Jim Gill sings about situations that make him sneeze. Your kids will automatically join in when they hear the group of kids on the recording make sneezing noises.

Picture Book: *A Sick Day for Amos McGee*

Amos McGee takes the number five bus to the zoo where he visits his animal friends. He plays chess with the elephant, races the tortoise (and lets the tortoise win), sits quietly with the penguin, lends a "handkerchief to the rhinoceros," and reads to the owl. One morning, Amos wakes up sick and stays home. The zoo animals miss him. They all board the number five bus and visit Amos. The elephant plays chess with Amos, the tortoise plays hide-and-seek (Amos is too tired to race), the penguin naps, the rhino provides Amos with a handkerchief, and the owl reads to Amos.

Storytelling Tips: Amos is a nice, gentle man. Match the story's tone by reading it with a gentle voice. It will help bring a welcome quiet moment to the story program as a whole.

Poem "Turning Into"

A kid hangs upside-down in a tree and hollers, "Wow!" The kid falls and the "Wow" turns into "Mom!" The poem takes ten seconds to read. The fun reaction from the audience takes a little longer.

Picture Book: *Bear Feels Sick*

Bear "feels achy with a stuffed-up nose." His friends—Hare, Mouse, Badger, Gopher, Mole, Raven, Owl, and Wren—try to help. They bring water, broth, and herbs. They also cover Bear with a quilt and sing lullabies. They watch him for hours. "We've done all we could." When Bear wakes up, he feels much better. Unfortunately, his friends feel sick. "You took care of me . . . now I'll take care of you."

Storytelling Tips: This is another gentle story. Read it in a relaxed voice. When Bear feels better, look happy. Look sad when his friends get sick. Nod your head when Bear declares he'll take care of his friends.

Movement Activity: "I Don't Feel Good"

Have the children sit down for this call-and-response activity. Instruct them to repeat what you say and imitate your motions.

I don't feel good.	I don't feel good.	(Make a face.)
Wiping my nose.	Wiping my nose.	(Mime wiping nose on left arm sleeve.)
Scratching an itch.	Scratching an itch.	(Scratch your body with your right hand.)

Drinking my medicine.	Drinking my medicine.	*(Hang tongue out of mouth.)*
Lying down to rest.	Lying down to rest.	*(Tip over to your side.)*
Falling asleep.	Falling asleep.	*(Close eyes. Snore softly.)*
(Pause a moment.)		
I feel great!	I feel great!	*(Open eyes and sit back up.)*
Time to play!	Time to play!	*(Throw arms overhead.)*

Picture Book with Felt Characters: *Felicity Floo Visits the Zoo*

Little Felicity Floo (who looks like a cast member of the old *Addams Family* show) visits the animals in the zoo even though she is sick. She wipes her "red, runny nose without a tissue" and proceeds to touch all of the animals, leaving behind "handprints of green residue." The animals get temperatures of "a hundred and two" and become "sluggish and sleepy and slightly subdued."

Storytelling Tips: Make felt characters of the animals mentioned in the story. You can find patterns on the Internet. Look in any search engine under "animal coloring pages." You may need to trace the rarer animals from the picture book itself. The 19 animals in the book include the following:

Blue-Footed Booby	Cockatoo	Elephant
Emu	Flamingo	Giraffe
Jabiru	Kangaroo	Lizard
Llama	Monkey	Mountain Goat
Ostrich	Owl	Panda
Peacock	Penguin	Toucan
Zebra		

Next, make several small green felt hands. Place these on the felt animals as Felicity Floo touches each animal in the book.

Song: "Mary Had a Little Cold"

Sing the following lyrics to the tune of "Mary Had a Little Lamb." Perform it as if you had a stuffed nose. Ask the children to join you as you sing it a second time. Encourage them to sing it with the "stuffed nose" vocal treatment.

Mary had a little cold, little cold, little cold.

Mary had a little cold, it's hard to sing this song.

'Cuz every time I try to sing, try to sing, try to sing,

Every time I try to sing, I (CHOO)-(CHOO)-(CHOO)-(CHOO)-(CHOO)!

Closing Picture Book: Pigs Make Me Sneeze!

This title in the popular Elephant & Piggie series finds Elephant sneezing in the presence of his best friend. Elephant assumes that he's allergic to pigs, "And Piggie is a pig!" Doctor Cat informs Elephant that he probably only has a cold. Elephant is delighted. "I am sick!!!" He runs back to Piggie only to find his friend sniffling and holding a box of tissues.

Storytelling Tips: Play up Elephant's sneezes. Put a series of the letter "A" before each "achoo." Read each "A" separately and make them louder and louder. The kids in the audience will join you. I get an extra laugh when I throw in a "boing" noise (not in the text) and point to the illustration of Piggie being spun around by the force of Elephant's sneeze. When you are finished reading the book, take the time to share the endpapers with the audience. The front endpapers show Elephant sneezing. The back endpapers not only show a sick Piggie, but also the Pigeon and Knuffle Bunny from Mo Willems's other popular series (Hyperion).

Tips for Back-up Books

- *Farm Flu.* Mom leaves her son alone on the farm for one day, and sure enough, that's the day one of the milk cows gets sick. The boy has never helped a sick cow before, so he puts the cow in a human bed, brings her hot alfalfa tea, and fluffs her pillows. Then the other animals get sick, so the boy brings them into the farmhouse, too. The animals take advantage of being pampered until the boy finally threatens to feed them mush.

  Storytelling Tips: As the boy gets worn-out caring for the animals, reflect this in your voice. At the end of the book, the boy, himself, gets the flu. Sound like you're sick when reading these lines.

- *Llama Llama Home with Mama.* Young Llama Llama is "feeling yucky, just not right." He has a fever and is told to head back to bed. He's not crazy about the taste of the medicine and is easily bored. Mama thinks of some activities for Llama Llama. Unfortunately, she also becomes sick. Llama Llama then reads to Mama.

  Storytelling Tips: When Llama Llama becomes tired of all of the sneezing, raise your volume as you read, "Soggy tissues, gobs of guck. Sniffing, snorting, sneezing, yuck!" Pause and then read the next line quietly. "Llama Llama, red pajama, sick and bored, at home with Mama." Be sure to show the kids the author's picture on the back flap. Anna Dewdney is seen in her pajamas, wiping her nose and holding a hot water bottle.

- *Sneeze, Big Bear, Sneeze.* The leaves fall off a tree when Big Bear sneezes. He thinks they fell because of his sneezing. While Big Bear is tacking the leaves back on the branches, the wind informs the bear that *she* was responsible for the leaves falling. Big Bear is not convinced. In fact, he feels his sneezing is why the apples fell to the ground and why the geese took flight. The wind finally gets mad and hollers. Big Bear runs home and the door slams behind him. "I know my sneeze didn't do that."

  Storytelling Tips: Cue the audience to sneeze when Big Bear sneezes. Also, when reading the wind's lines, have a peaceful, sensible vocal delivery. When wind loses her cool, shout her angry line, "I'm tired of this crazy, ridiculous stuff. I'm the Autumn Breeze!"

All You Need Is Love

Final Lesson Plan

1. Opening Picture Book: *Mr. Pusskins: A Love Story* by Sam Lloyd. Atheneum, 2006.
2. Musical Activity: "There's a Little Wheel A-Turning," traditional.
3. Picture Book: *And I Love You* by Ruth Krauss. Illustrated by Steven Kellogg. Scholastic, 2010.
4. Movement Activity: "But Mostly I Love You" by Rob Reid.
5. Picture Book/Creative Movement: *I Love You Through and Through* by Bernadette Rossetti-Shustak. Illustrated by Caroline Jayne Church. Scholastic, 2005.
6. Movement Activity: "Easy-Peasy" by Rob Reid.
7. Picture Book: *My Heart Is Like a Zoo* by Michael Hall. Greenwillow Books, 2010.
8. Closing Craft Project: Make a Heart-Shaped Animal.

How I Got There

Initial Inspiration

Many times, a lesson plan is built around a specific song. In this case, "All You Need Is Love" by the Beatles (Magical Mystery Tour, EMI, 1967) inspired this theme. There are many possibilities one could take with the word "love." There is the love one feels for a parent or other family members, and vice versa. One can love oneself (this could segue into an exploration of "self-esteem" resources). There is our love of the world around us, and loving life, itself. As you consider how you might customize this theme, kids can be interviewed ahead of time and asked what they love. The responses may include pets, toys, and friends. These topics can also be worked into the program.

The Scavenger Hunt

I used the word "love" in both subject and word searches. There were several hits; almost too many. Most of the picture books in this category were very similar to each other; they consisted of dialogue between a parent and a child about how much they loved each other. One such book followed by another, over and over, could lead to a boring program. Further searching in titles yielded a little more variety on the term "love." There are love stories that feature animals. Some books had a fun twist on the word, such as *Love You When You Whine*. When I located *My Heart is Like a Zoo*, I knew I would limit the program to just four picture books. *My Heart is Like a Zoo* dovetails so well into a craft project that I couldn't resist it, and mixing crafts with young children takes up a bit of time.

The Choices

- *And I Love You* by Ruth Krauss is a nice, quiet book with fun illustrations by Steven Kellogg.
- *I Love You Through and Through* by Bernadette Rossetti-Shustak has great potential for audience participation with movement.
- *Mr. Pusskins; A Love Story* by Sam Lloyd is a funny book with an animal twist on the word "love." The sequel, *Mr. Pusskins and Little Whiskers: Another Love Story* (Atheneum, 2008) was considered—the two books could have been set up as "bookends" to the program. However, the inclusion of the lengthy craft activity was the deciding factor in my not including the sequel.
- *My Heart Is Like a Zoo* is splashy and colorful, with that natural follow-up craft project possibility.

Back-up Books Selection

- *Guess How Much I Love You* by Sam McBratney and illustrated by Anita Jeram (Candlewick Press, 1994) is one of the most popular parent-child relationship books on the market. It has movement potential similar to that of *I Love You Through and Through*.
- *Love You When You Whine* by Emily Jenkins and illustrated by Sergio Ruzzier (Farrar, Straus and Giroux, 2006) has a fun twist with that kid-appealing whine factor. I would have added this title to the final lesson plan as the fifth book had there not been a craft activity.
- *Woof: a Love Story* by Sarah Weeks and illustrated by Holly Berry (HarperCollins, 2009) is another fun animal love story.

Choosing the Order of the Picture Books

It made sense to end the program with a craft idea connected to the book, *My Heart is Like a Zoo*. *I Love You Through and Through* is very short and can be acted out by the audience, so that went next-to-last in the lineup. For me, it was a toss-up which of the other two books should open the program. In the end, the pictures of grumpy Mr. Pusskins made me laugh, and I thought it would get everyone's attention. That placement left the second spot open for *And I Love You*.

Locating and Creating the In-Between Activities

Looking for love songs in the usual music resources turned up the traditional song, "There's a Little Wheel A-Turning," found on the recording *Wee Sing Fun 'n' Folk* (Price Stern Sloan, 1989). The accompanying booklet has the score for those who are so musically inclined. The motions in the Wee Sing version were altered a bit for this program.

Next, the traditional musical activity "Skinnamarink" made popular by Sharon, Lois, and Bram (Great Big Hits #2, Casablanca Kids, 2004) came to mind. Kids enjoy making the motions of pointing to their eyes, then their hearts, and then to another person when singing the lyrics "I love you." I started scribbling some words on paper to create a similar type of movement verse and came up with "But Mostly I Love You."

The overall program still needed one more in-between activity. When my grandson Parker was three, we made each other laugh by saying, "That was easy-peasy" over and over. I thought of other simple things a small child could take pride in doing and, within a few minutes, I had the final ditty "Easy-Peasy."

Program Presentation

Opening Picture Book: Mr. Pusskins: a Love Story

Emily loves her cat, Mr. Pusskins, but the feline decides to look for different adventures. "He went to places he wasn't meant to go and did things he wasn't meant to do." He finds that being naughty is a lot of fun. But eventually, the appeal of his new life diminishes. Mr. Pusskins aches to have someone say that she loves him. He learns that Emily has made lost posters about him, and he contacts her on the phone. "'Meow,' whimpered Mr. Pusskins in a very sad little voice." The two friends are reunited.

Storytelling Tips: There are slight mood changes in the text that your voice can reflect. The book can open with a cheery description of Emily and her cat. The mood shifts as Mr. Pusskins leaves and becomes naughty. It changes again when he becomes worried. At the end, your voice can return to a cheery delivery.

Musical Activity: "There's a Little Wheel A-Turning"

"There's a little wheel a-turning in my heart,	(*Roll hands over each other and then point to heart.*)
There's a little wheel a-turning in my heart.	(*Repeat motions.*)
In my heart,	(*With pointer finger, make a circle over your heart.*)
In my heart,	(*Repeat motion.*)
There's a little wheel a-turning in my heart."	(*Repeat first motions.*)

Picture Book: *And I Love You*

This story was originally published as *Big and Little* in 1987, and has been updated with new illustrations by Steven Kellogg. The simple text compares large objects and concepts with smaller counterparts. "Big forests love little trees. Big fields love little flowers." A cat and her kitten go on an imaginary journey. The mother cat is actually reading the same story we are reading.

Storytelling Tips: The page layout throughout the book is executed well so that the reader shares the first part of the sentence, allows the audience to see the accompanying picture, and then turns the page to read the second half of the line. Just let the book do the work.

Movement Activity: "But Mostly I Love You"

(Have everyone stand.)

"I love, I love the earth below,	*(Touch the ground.)*
I love the sky so blue,	*(Point upward.)*
I love this world so very much,	*(Head back, face upward, arms out, spin slowly in a circle.)*
But mostly I love you."	*(Point to eyes on "I," point to your heart on "love," and point to someone else on "you.")*

Picture Book/Creative Movement: *I Love You Through and Through*

The book starts with the title phrase and continues with "I love your top side. I love your bottom side." The little boy in the book makes motions and facial expressions when told, "I love you" inside and outside, as well as "your silly sad and your mad side." There are many similar examples scattered throughout the text. The book ends with, "I love you through and through yesterday, today, and tomorrow, too."

Storytelling Tips: Ask the audience to act out each line as you read the book. The children can make expressions when "happy and sad" appear. Encourage them to run in place during "I love you running." The funniest moves will be "I love your top side . . ." when they pat their heads, and, "I love your bottom side," when they imitate the boy in the book who is showing us his rear end.

Movement Activity: "Easy-Peasy"

(Have everyone stand.)

"You can clap,	*(Clap)*
You can clap,	*(Clap)*
Why, that's so easy-peasy	*(Give a thumbs-up motion.)*
You can smile,	*(Give a big smile and keep it going for next verse.)*
You can smile,	
That's easy-peasy, too.	*(Wave hand as if saying "That was nothing.")*
You can sing,	*(Stroke throat with mouth open. Sing these three lines.)*
You can sing,	
Why, that's so easy-peasy.	*(Give a thumbs-up motion.)*
You can love,	*(Cross hands over heart.)*
You can love,	
That's easy-peasy, too."	*(Wave hand as if saying "That was nothing.")*

Picture Book: *My Heart Is Like a Zoo*

Different zoo animals designed with construction paper hearts are featured in this book. Each animal reflects a different aspect of love. "Steady as a yak, silly as a seal." The book opens with the title line and ends with "tired as a zookeeper who's had a busy day." We see the "zookeeper" (a child) sleeping in bed with the various animals shown to be toys.

Storytelling Tips: Have fun with your voice reflecting the different moods of love as they appear in the story. "Angry as a bear" can be read in an angry voice, while "frightened as a rabbit" can be high-pitched and fearful. This book leads to the closing craft project.

Closing Craft Project: Make a Heart-Shaped Animal

As someone who is not into crafts, I wanted to make this project as simple as possible. I showed the kids the image of the seal from the book. As you will see from the illustration, the seal is made of one large heart-shape for the body, and three little hearts for the feet and tail. There are two small black circles for the eye and nose, and one large circle for the ball balanced on the seal's nose. Cut out several of these paper shapes ahead of time, and place them on a table with glue sticks and sheets of construction paper. Encourage the kids to make their own seals. My craft-oriented friends were much more ambitious when they heard about this project, and they provided many heart shapes of all colors and sizes for the kids—as well as rectangles for legs and triangles for beaks and horns. If you are so inclined, I encourage providing all this, because it enabled the kids to make any animal they wanted.

Tips for Back-up Books

- *Love You When You Whine.* A mother assures her youngster that she will love her child even when the child is not on her best behavior. We see the little one pulling the phone cord while the mother is talking, pouring cereal on the floor, painting the walls (and the dog), tracking mud into the house, throwing up on mom's good wool coat, spreading jam on the computer, and much, much more.

  Storytelling Tips: Put a little beat between reading each spread. Each page features its own example of being naughty. Don't sound cheerful while reading, but let your vocals express one's efforts to be patient. The page that gets the biggest laughs (at least from any adults in the audience) is the one where "you scream 'Lollipop lollipop lollipop' for forty-five minutes in line at the bank."

- *Guess How Much I Love You.* Little Nutbrown Hare tells Big Nutbrown Hare, "Guess how much I love you." Little Nutbrown Hare then holds out his arms as long as they reach and says, "This much." Big Nutbrown Hare does the same thing but his reach is longer. Little Nutbrown Hare proceeds to demonstrate his love by reaching high, tumbling upside down, hopping, and finally, pointing to the moon and saying, "I love you right up to the moon" before falling asleep. Big Nutbrown Hare whispers back, "I love you right up to the moon—and back."

  Storytelling Tips: Let the children stretch their arms and hop along with Little Nutbrown Hare. Have a paper construction moon hanging in one corner of the story program area. When Little Nutbrown Hare talks about the moon, the kids can point to it and then pretend they are falling asleep.

- *Woof: a Love Story.* "A dog is a dog and a cat is a cat, and most of the time it's as simple as that." Not in this case. A dog spots a cat and falls in love with her. When he says, "I love you," the cat hears, "woof woof woof woof" and is frightened. She climbs a tree. The dog is frustrated that the cat doesn't understand him. He digs up a bone (it's actually a trombone, which he plays to express his feelings). The cat now understands the dog's feelings and returns his love.

  Storytelling Tips: There is a nice lilt to the verse text. Give the dog's dialogue a low masculine voice and give the cat's vocal delivery a higher pitched feminine feel. One fun line is, "He turned and he left, with his ears hanging low." I pause here and wink at the audience (who don't always get the nod to the song lyric, but that's okay).

Go Green!

Final Lesson Plan

1. Opening Song: "Keep it Green" by Bill Harley from *Big Big World* (A&M, 1993).
2. Picture Book: *The Umbrella* by Jan Brett. Putnam, 2004.
3. Musical Activity: "Three Green Parrots," traditional. New words by Rob Reid.
4. Picture Book: *Nibbles: A Green Tale* by Charlotte Middleton. Marshall Cavendish, 2009.
5. Movement Activity: "Red Light, Green Light," traditional.
6. Picture Book with Felt Characters: *Quiet in the Garden* by Aliki. Greenwillow Books, 2009.
7. Poem: "Grass" by George Shannon from *Busy in the Garden*. Illustrated by Sam Williams. Greenwillow Books, 2006.
8. Picture Book: *Katy Did It!* by Lorianne Siomades. Boyds Mill Press, 2009.
9. Musical Activity: "Katydid," traditional. New words by Rob Reid.
10. Poem: "Zucchini" by George Shannon from *Busy in the Garden*. Illustrated by Sam Williams. Greenwillow Books, 2006.
11. Closing Picture Book: *Monsters Don't Eat Broccoli* by Barbara Jean Hicks. Illustrated by Sue Hendra. Knopf, 2009.

How I Got There

Initial Inspiration

It can be fun to conduct programs that feature concepts such as colors. However, I haven't found enough general color concept books with interesting enough storylines to fill a whole program. The search has to include another aspect of color—in this case, I chose the color green. Green, today, is closely associated with the environment. After an initial search of picture books dealing with the environment, I decided to further broaden the potential field and include other objects and characters that are green.

The Scavenger Hunt

Both subject and word searches for "Environment" brought up a few possible choices, but not enough to make an exciting story program. Fortunately, if you type "things that are green" in any Internet search engine, several lists pop up. These lists include other aspects of the environment, which in turn, leads to more searches and more desirable hits in the form of quality, program-friendly picture books. My findings centered on the topics of trees and other plants, gardens, and Earth Day. These all fell under the umbrella term, "things that are green."

Other subjects and characters from the lists were lumped into other groups. Green animals made up the second group: Frogs, snakes, turtles, lizards, green insects, and green birds. A third group featured green imaginary characters, like leprechauns, dragons, witches, and monsters. The last group consisted of green food: Limes, apples, lettuce, cabbage, celery, watermelon, spinach, asparagus, green beans, peas, and, of course, green eggs and ham. All of these possibilities made for a promising and fun lesson plan. To balance things out, I ultimately decided to select one or two books connected to the environmental theme, and then have a representative animal book, an imaginary creature book, and a food book.

The Choices

Selecting the lineup for this story program was not cut-and-dry. The original lineup I created included the following picture books:

- *A Cold Winter's Good Knight* by Shelley Moore Thomas and illustrated by Jennifer Plecas (Dutton, 2008), a cute story about little dragons (imaginary characters).
- *Do Not Build a Frankenstein* by Neil Numberman (Greenwillow Books, 2009), a funny book with a green monster (imaginary characters).
- *Nibbles: A Green Tale* by Charlotte Middleton (Marshall Cavendish, 2009), has a nice, breezy storyline (environmental/plant categories).
- *This Tree Counts* by Alison Formento and illustrated by Sarah Snow (Albert Whitman, 2010) is a quiet, reflective environmental book.
- *Too Many Frogs* by Ann and John Hassett (Houghton Mifflin, 2011) is another funny story representing green animals.

As I began to put the books in order, I had second thoughts. There were too many imaginary creature books and not as many environment-related books as originally intended. It was time to go back to the scavenger hunt results. *The Umbrella* by Jan Brett has a lot of green color on every page and warranted another look. Upon re-reading the book, I felt the cumulative pattern of the text made it flow nicely. It was worth the time to share it with the kids.

With the longer *Umbrella* book in, I opted to cut the lengthier *Too Many Frogs* and replace it with *Katy Did It,* a shorter animal book. A second look at *The Quiet Garden* sparked the idea to use felt characters with it, and so this book replaced *This Tree Counts* as an environmental choice. Finally, after re-discovering that *Monsters Don't Eat Broccoli* not only had the imaginary creature component, but it also had the missing food element and an environmental element, too, I put it into the line-up. With that addition, I felt there was no room for the other imaginary creature books *(Do Not Build a Frankenstein* and *A Cold Winter's Good Knight)*. These last two books, as well as *Too Many Frogs,* were selected as back-up books, instead.

This final collection of picture books, for some reason, seemed to have a more cohesive feel than the first batch did. It can be healthy to practice a trial-and-error approach and move things around when something doesn't feel right.

Back-up Books Selection

- *Too Many Frogs*
- *A Cold Winter's Good Knight*
- *Do Not Build a Frankenstein*

Choosing the Order of the Picture Books

Once the "dust settled" regarding my final picture book choices, designing the order went fast. The longest text, *The Umbrella,* went first, followed by *Nibbles: A Green Story. Quiet in the Garden* was placed third because, as the title suggests, it provides a quiet time in the program. The other animal story, *Katy Did It,* came fourth; and *Monsters Don't Eat Broccoli* rounded up the line-up.

Locating and Creating the In-Between Activities

Children's Jukebox, 2nd edition, has several songs listed under the "Ecology/Nature" entries. "Keep It Green" by Bill Harley was chosen because of the emphasis on the color green. Instead of being a featured song in the program, I opted to play it for children as they enter the program area.

The Wee Sing recordings proved to be a wonderful source for this topic. Three nature and animal-related songs were chosen. The traditional song, "Three Blue Pigeons," from *Wee Sing Children's Songs and Fingerplays* (Price Stern Sloan, 1977) caught my eye because of the color reference. It was easy to look over the lyrics and change the blue pigeons to green parrots, a bird found in the tropics. This change made the song a good choice to be paired with *The Umbrella*. The camp song "Grasshopper" from *Wee Sing Silly Songs* (Price Stern Sloan, 1982) is sung to the tune of "The Battle Hymn of the Republic." Once again, it worked to make small alterations to fit the theme. The grasshoppers were changed to katydids so the song could go along with *Katy Did It*.

Finally, "Red Light, Green Light" appears in the booklet that accompanies the recording *Wee Sing Games, Games, Games* (Price Stern Sloan, 1998). The game instructs the children to run when the leader yells, "Green light," and stop when the leader yells, "Red light." I didn't want the audience to run around wildly in the program area, so I decided to do a quiet, whispering version of the game. This became a nice set-up activity for the picture book, *Quiet in the Garden*.

In the end, I felt the program needed something else. It was time to paw through the library's poetry section. *Busy in the Garden* by George Shannon turned up. Each poem in this picture book has something to do with gardening, making it perfect for a "Go Green" theme. Two humorous poems, "Grass" and "Zucchini," were chosen, and the line-up was complete.

Program Presentation

Opening Song: "Keep It Green"

As the children enter the program area, play this song in the background. Harly sings, "You got to keep it green/ You got to keep it clean/ You know just what I mean/ You got to keep it green." The next verse implores the listener to "keep it blue." He describes how some people make "this old earth dirty," but we're going to show we care. This is a nice segue to the first picture book.

Picture Book: *The Umbrella*

Carlos goes into the green forest and sets his umbrella down on the ground. While he's climbing the tall fig tree, a tiny tree frog hops into the umbrella. When a fig falls into the umbrella, a toucan joins the frog. A kinkajou is the next animal to climb in. A baby tapir tumbles in, followed by a Quetzal bird. A monkey throws the umbrella and its inhabitants into the river. He then climbs in. A jaguar follows. When tiny hummingbird sets down on the umbrella, it "tumbles over, and everyone falls out." Carlos climbs back down and wonders why he didn't see any animals.

Storytelling Tips: I thought about using a different voice for each animal, but it got too complicated. It worked well just using my normal voice. Frog has a few Spanish phrases, so be aware of them before reading.

Musical Activity: "Three Green Parrots"

Have three children sit on chairs in the front of the room. They can leave one by one as the song dictates, and return to the chairs one by one. If some children are upset they didn't get to act out the role of the parrots, tell them that they have an important part, too. They can say 'Oh-oh-oh' and 'Whee-ee-ee' very loudly. If you have a small group, say ten kids in the audience, add enough verses to have "Ten Green Parrots" and let them all act as parrots. This is an easy song to chant if you don't have access to the recording.

Three green parrots sitting in a tree,

Three green parrots sitting in a tree,

One flew away! Oh-oh-oh! *(One child leaves.)*

Two green parrots sitting in a tree,

Two green parrots sitting in a tree,

One flew away! Oh-oh-oh! *(Second child leaves.)*

One green parrot sitting in a tree,

One green parrot sitting in a tree,

One flew away! Oh-oh-oh! *(Third child leaves.)*

No green parrots sitting in a tree,

No green parrots sitting in a tree,

One flew back! Whee-ee-ee-ee! *(One child returns.)*

One green parrot sitting in a tree,

One green parrot sitting in a tree,

One flew back! Whee-ee-ee-ee! *(Second child returns.)*

Two green parrots sitting in a tree,

Two green parrots sitting in a tree,

One flew back! Whee-ee-ee-ee! *(Third child returns.)*

Three green parrots sitting in a tree,

Three green parrots sitting in a tree,

Hooray, horray, hooray, horray!

Picture Book: *Nibbles: A Green Tale*

Nibbles, a guinea pig, loves to eat dandelion leaves. But so do the other guinea pigs living in Dandeville. Soon, the "dandelion leaves began to run out," and the guinea pigs have to make do with cabbage. But Nibbles finds a single dandelion growing outside his bedroom window. He goes to the library and does some research. It pays off. When the dandelion grows a "beautiful white head of tiny seeds," Nibbles takes it to a hill and "the seeds filled the air." Soon, there are dandelions all over. "Dandeville was filled with the happy sound of munching once more."

Storytelling Tips: There are two times when the residents of Dandeville make munching and nibbling noises. Before you start reading, instruct your audience to make eating noises at the appropriate times in the book.

Movement Activity: "Red Light Green Light"

Instruct the children to tiptoe around the room very quietly when you whisper "green light," and to freeze in place when you whisper "red light." After a few minutes of allowing the children to move around, instruct them to go back to their sitting spots on "green light." Once there, they should rock gently back and forth until the final "red light." This quiet activity will make a nice transition to the next picture book.

Picture Book with Felt Characters: *Quiet in the Garden*

A young child loves to observe nature in the garden. "If I am very still, I see more." A robin flies down to nibble berries. A snail eats leaves. A butterfly sips nectar. A "worm squiggles in the soil." A squirrel eats an acorn. A spider catches a fly. A turtle munches moss. A lizard eats a moth. A frog catches a gnat. A fish nibbles algae. A mouse finds food in the compost heap, and a rabbit eats a leaf. In the end, the child gathers food from the green garden.

Storytelling Tips: Make felt characters of the 12 animals from the patterns on pages 74–77 and display them as each appears in the story. Before you begin reading, ask the children to sit very still and listen very carefully to the sounds around them. Start reading in a quiet voice to match the tone of the book.

Poem: "Grass"

This is a short poem with a funny visual at the end. The green grass grows and grows and is mowed and mowed and mowed until one day, the child exclaims "Oh! Snow!"

Picture Book: *Katy Did It!*

Katy, a green katydid, hops on a flower and scatters pollen everywhere. This makes a bee angry. She then hops on tomatoes and scares the aphids. Katy's hopping also tangles up a spider's web. In the end, her hopping abilities save some ants trapped in their anthill.

Storytelling Tips: Every time Katy hops, the reader says, "Boing, Boing, Boing." Have the kids say it with you and make hopping motions with their fingers.

Musical Activity: "Katydid"

Sing this camp song to the tune of "The Battle Hymn of the Republic." Instruct the children to wiggle the first two fingers of their left hand and have them "jump" over their right hand. The two first fingers on the right hand can wiggle throughout the rhyme, also.

The first katydid jumped over the second katydid's back,

Oh, the first katydid jumped over the second katydid's back,

The first katydid jumped over the second katydid's back,

It jumped and jumped and jumped.

They were only playing leapfrog,

They were only playing leapfrog,

They were only playing leapfrog,

When the first katydid jumped.

Poem: "Zucchini"

This poem starts with "Zucchini/meeny/miney/moe" and talks about how a zucchini seed can lead to a lot of zucchini. The rest of the poem is a fun, long litany of zucchini possibilities from "Zucchini bread" to "Zucchini hash/and succotash."

Closing Picture Book: *Monsters Don't Eat Broccoli*

We learn that monsters don't like eating broccoli, nor other green vegetables like artichokes and lima beans. They do like eating trees as well as boulders, rockets, and tractors. The children at the end of the story pretend their broccoli is really "crunchy, munchy trees," and they ask for "another helping, please."

Storytelling Tips: Give the audience a confused look whenever the monsters eat a non-food item.

Tips for Back-up Books

- *Too Many Frogs.* Nana Quimby has a terrible time dealing with green frogs in her house. Ten frogs hop up from the cellar. A little girl advises Nana Quimby to put the frogs in a goldfish bowl. Next, twenty frogs hop up from the cellar. A boy advises Nana Quimby to put the frogs in cups of water. More and more frogs show up and various children help Nana Quimby decide what to do with them. After a million frogs arrive, Nana Quimby decides to flood the cellar with water and let the frogs hang out there.

Storytelling Tips: Every time Nana Quimby rushes to the window, she cries, "Too many frogs!" Have the kids chime this repetitive phrase with Nana Quimby.

- *Do Not Build a Frankenstein!* The new kid warns other children to not build a Frankenstein monster. When he did, his Frankenstein became downright annoying. "He'll chase away your friends and your pets and he'll break all your toys." Things got so bad that the boy felt compelled to run away and start a life in a new town. Of course, his Frankenstein finds him. The other children join the green monster for a game of Monster Tag. The new kid pauses and then says, "Hey! Wait for me!"

  Storytelling Tips: It's fun to read the new kid's lines with an excited, breathless, panicked delivery.

- *A Cold Winter's Good Knight.* The Good Knight finds the three small green dragons shivering in their cave. He takes them to the ball at the castle and warns them to mind their manners. The dragons cause a ruckus. They blow their fiery breath on the fire and smoke fills the castle. They swing from the chandelier and contemplate other adventures. The Good Knight finally realizes that the little dragons don't know what manners are. They are sorry. "We did not mean to ruin the ball." They start saying "please" and "thank you."

  Storytelling Tips: The three dragons speak in a series of threes. Give each dragon a distinctive voice for comedic effect.

Shh! Be Quiet! Stories and Activities about Noises

Final Lesson Plan

1. Opening Song: "Hello" by Miss Jackie from *Peanut Butter, Tarzan, and Roosters* (Miss Jackie, 1981).
2. Picture Book: *The Quiet Book* by Deborah Underwood. Illustrated by Renata Liwska. Houghton Mifflin, 2010.
3. Musical Activity: "Scat Like That" by Greg and Steve from *On the Move* (Youngheart, 1983).
4. Picture Book: *Too Much Noise in the Library* by Susan Margaret Chapman. Illustrated by Abby Carter. UpstartBooks, 2010.
5. Sound Effects Activity: "Shh! Shh!" by Rob Reid.
6. Picture Book: *Push Button* by Aliki. Greenwillow Books, 2010.
7. Musical Activity: "Boom! Boom! Ain't It Great to be Crazy?" traditional.
8. Picture Book: *Cows to the Rescue* by John Himmelman. Henry Holt & Company, 2011.
9. Closing Picture Book: *The Loud Book!* by Deborah Underwood. Illustrated by Renata Liwska. Houghton Mifflin, 2011.

How I Got There

Initial Inspiration

Sound effects in any story program are fun. They are usually interactive and help keep the audience involved for the duration of the program. Most of my programs have some aspect of sound effects. This time, the whole program is built upon that notion. This program is designed to start out quietly, then build up the noise level bit by bit to the loudest activities and books at the end.

The Scavenger Hunt

Thank you, Library of Congress, for the subject heading, "Noise." Some of the titles I found came from this subject search, including Underwood's *The Loud Book!* When I discovered this book had a companion called *The Quiet Book* (which for some reason didn't appear under the "Noise" subject search), it was natural these two should bookend the entire program. One of the subject headings for *The Quiet Book* was "Quietude!" (Who knew?) There's also a subject heading for "Animal Sounds" in the catalogue. A few more titles were located by using the following search terms: "Sounds," "Loud," "Snoring," and "Shh."

The Choices

- *Cows to the Rescue* is a pattern story that will encourage the audience to yell the title phrase over and over.
- *The Loud Book!* is a natural fit for a noise theme program.
- *Push Button* by Aliki has multiple sound effects throughout the book.
- *The Quiet Book* by Deborah Underwood is a nice contrast to most sound effect books because it emphasizes soft, gentle noises.
- *Too Much Noise in the Library* by Susan Margaret Chapman is set in a library and focuses on the great debate: Should the library be quiet or noisy?

Back-up Books Selection

- *Farmyard Beat* by Lindsey Craig and illustrated by Marc Brown (Knopf, 2011) has a rap-like flow to the text along with animal noises.
- *Shhh!* by Valeri Gorbachev (Philomel Books, 2011) is a good option that came up when I searched the word, "shh."
- *Shout! Shout It Out!* by Denise Fleming (Henry Holt & Company, 2011) illustrates pictures of children with their mouths wide open as they shout out familiar objects and concepts.

Choosing the Order of the Picture Books

As stated before, the program is bookended by the two Underwood books, with the noisier and more active *The Loud Book!* placed at the end. *Too Much Noise in the Library* has the longest text and goes second. *The Cows to the Rescue* has a fairly short text and is also noisy; so I placed it just before the final picture book, leaving *Push Button* for the middle of the program plan.

Locating and Creating the "In-Between" Activities

The thought of kids shushing each other, as well as the stereotype of a librarian shushing patrons, led to the development of an original activity. I made a list of places and situations in which one would want to be quiet: church, school, a recital/play/concert, naptime, trying not to scare or startle an animal, and of course, the library. The library was initially placed in the first verse, but after coming up with the other scenarios, it was moved to the end of the piece. An online rhyming dictionary helped a lot. While the finished version sounds a little forced, the kids have so much fun making the shushing noises, they don't notice. This pairs well with the book *Too Much Noise in the Library*.

Miss Jackie's recording *Peanut Butter, Tarzan, and Roosters* has a great version of Ella Jenkins's famous song, "Hello." Simply play the recording, let Miss Jackie sing, and then react to her directions. Since it's a hello song, it gets the program off on a good start.

Finally, instead of going to *Children's Jukebox*, I went to my book, *Something Musical Happened at the Library* (ALA Editions, 2007). It contains a list of "call-and-response" songs that are good for a sound effect lesson plan. The traditional song, "Boom! Boom! Ain't It Great to be Crazy?" will encourage kids to pound the floor every time they hear the words, "Boom! Boom!" This song is loud, so I placed it near the end of the line-up. A second song located in the "call-and-response" list was "Scat Like That" by Greg and Steve. Again, play the recording and let the performers lead your audience. Since it's the quieter of these two songs, it goes near the beginning of the program.

Program Presentation

Opening Song: "Hello"

After everyone is seated, play the recording without saying a word. Miss Jackie is heard with her own audience of children. As she directs her audience, stand in front of your kids and direct them silently with your hands. Miss Jackie tells half of the group to wave to the other half as they follow the simple lyrics. The other group responds with their own waves. While this is going on, divide your group with your hands and then indicate when one group waves and then when the other group waves back. Miss Jackie continues the silliness by having the children wave their pinkie fingers, elbows, heads, and tongues. The song concludes with the kids shaking hands and then hugging. Mime all of those actions so your kids will follow suit. Once the song is done, you can talk, explaining that even though you didn't speak at first, this program is all about noises.

Picture Book: *The Quiet Book*

Several woodland animals explain that there are "many kinds of quiet." These range from "first one awake quiet" to "sound asleep quiet." In between are examples of "sleeping sister quiet," "make a wish quiet," and "first look at your new haircut quiet."

Storytelling Tips: Show the cover to your young audience so it can see the four characters making a shushing motion. Show the kids the back cover where a bear cub says, "Sssssshhhhhhhh! This is The Quiet Book." Read the entire book slowly and in a quiet voice. Make a fist-pump and an accompanying silent "Yes!" when you read "Story time quiet."

Musical Activity: "Scat Like That"

Greg and Steve lead the audience with a call-and-response series of musical phrases, such as "Dooby-dooby-dooby," "Uh-uh-uh," and "Doot-doot-n-do-wop." The kids also sing the title phrase a few times and will probably sway back and forth as they sing.

Picture Book: *Too Much Noise in the Library*

Ms. Reade, the school librarian, runs a successful, yet noisy, library, The DVDs blare, the teachers chatter, the children giggle, and Adam asks a million questions. One day, the mayor visits the library. He's bothered by the noise. "Something must be done about this!" He starts getting rid of the noisy aspects of the library one by one, ending with Adam being sent back to the classroom. Ms. Reade convinces him that it's too quiet and he agrees. Bit by bit, the joyful noises return to the library.

Storytelling Tips: Before you start reading this book, whisper to the kids that the library is nice and quiet. However, here's a story about a noisy library. Revert to a slightly noisier reading voice. Also, take note of the many sound effects on most pages of this book. "Every day the book return thumped, kerplop kerplop, the computer keys tapped, clickety click, the printers screeched zipped zing," and so on. The children will learn the sound effects quickly. Pause a beat after each example to let the kids recite them.

Sound Activity: "Shh! Shh!"

Instruct the children to put their finger to their lip and say "Shh! Shh!" after you recite each line.

What do we say when teacher's talking in school? Shh! Shh!

What do we say when we're trying to look cool? Shh! Shh!

What do we say when someone's trying to sleep? Shh! Shh!

What do we say when Dad says "Don't make a peep!" Shh! Shh!

What do we say in the library? Shh! Shh!

Unless we're in storytime!

Hip! Hip! Hooray! *(Have the audience pump their fists and repeat, "Hip! Hip! Hooray!")*

Picture Book: *Push Button*

A little boy loves to push buttons. He finds buttons on the telephone, the elevator, the vacuum cleaner, and the television remote. Whenever he pushes a button, there is a corresponding sound. When he hurts his finger, he "takes a rest" and starts looking at books. This inspires him to do other activities that don't involve pushing a button, like painting and playing outdoors. These new activities, however, still create sounds.

Storytelling Tips: Because there are multiple sound effects written throughout the book, read the text slowly and pause to let the kids make the sound effect immediately after you read it. The bright, colorful fonts used for the sound effects make it nearly impossible not to make the noises. Some examples, such as pushing the button, don't have the sound effect written in the text. You might want to add one, such as "ding." The first double-page spread has over a dozen sound effects. Take your time, read them all, and let the kids repeat them back to you.

Musical Activity: "Boom! Boom! Ain't It Great to Be Crazy?"

This nonsense song has been around for years. Sing it yourself or find a recording to play. The song can be found on the following recordings: *Corner Grocery Store* by Raffi (Troubador, 1979) *Nancy Cassidy's Kidssongs* by Nancy Cassidy (Klutz Press, 2004), and *Wee Sing Silly Songs* by Pamela Beall and Susan Nipp (Price Stern Sloan, 1982). Every time the children hear, "Boom! Boom!", instruct them to clap their hands or beat on the floor.

A horse and a flea and three blind mice

Sat on a curbstone shooting dice,

The horse he slipped and fell on the flea,

"Whoops," said the flea, "There's a horse on me!"

Boom! Boom! Ain't it great to be crazy?

Boom! Boom! Ain't it great to be crazy?

Giddy and foolish the whole day through,

Boom! Boom! Ain't it great to be crazy?

Way down South where bananas grow,

A flea stepped on an elephant's toe,

The elephant cried, with tears in his eyes,

"Why don't you pick on someone your own size?"

Boom! Boom! Ain't it great to be crazy?

Boom! Boom! Ain't it great to be crazy?

Giddy and foolish the whole day through,

Boom! Boom! Ain't it great to be crazy?

Picture Book: *Cows to the Rescue*

A herd of cows keeps showing up to help the Greenstalk family. When the car doesn't start, the cows give the family members rides to the county fair. When Ernie the duck gets muddy before the Handsomest Duck Contest, the cows clean him up. When Emily is too afraid to go on the Ferris wheel by herself, the cows join her (and a couple of the cows are not too crazy about being so high in the sky). This is the sequel to the hilarious books *Chickens to the Rescue* (Henry Holt & Company, 2006) and *Pigs to the Rescue* (Henry Holt & Company, 2010).

Storytelling Tips: Each time there is a disaster, the cows arrive with the text blaring, "Cows to the rescue!" Let the kids belt it out.

Closing Picture Book: *The Loud Book!*

The animals from *The Quiet Book* are back and this time they are noisy. They explain that "there are lots of louds," and they demonstrate them. There's "alarm clock loud" to get us started in the day. There's "walking to school loud," "burp during quiet time loud," and dropping your lunch tray loud." After school, there's "parade in the park loud," "Aunt Tillie's banjo band loud," and "crackling campfire loud." Finally, there's "snoring sister loud" and "cricket loud" as we try to go to sleep.

Storytelling Tips: After you read each example of "loudness," pause and let the kids give their vocal interpretations. Some of Underwood's examples are fairly abstract for preschoolers. "Unexpected entrance loud" shows characters in a play rushing onto the stage. Whatever noise they can contribute will be just fine.

Tips for Back-up Books

- *Farmyard Beat.* "Chicks can't sleep 'cause they got that beat!" And if the chicks are making a lot of peeping noises, they keep sheep awake. The sheep get "the beat" and make their own racket. This is turn wakes and activates cat, cows, dog, and finally Farmer Sue. They all pause and then start up making noises again until finally they fall asleep.

  Storytelling Tips: This would be a fun choral reading with some coworkers to present to the children. The first voice can read, "Chicks can't sleep." The second voice reads, "Chicks can't sleep." The third voice reads, "Chicks can't sleep." All three voices say the next line. "Cause they got that beat!" The first voice then reads, "Peep! Peep! Peep-peep-peep!" The first and second voices read the next line. "Peep! Peep! Peep-peep-peep!" The third voice reads, "All that peeping wakes up . . ." All three voices say "Sheep!" Continue this pattern throughout the book. When the pattern breaks up, simply divide the rest of the lines among the three voices. Have all three voices say the last word together in a quiet voice. "Asleep."

- *Shout! Shout It Out!* Children in the book are encouraged to shout out numbers one through ten. They move on to shouting out the alphabet, colors, familiar birds and animals, and different vehicles.

  Storytelling Tips: The numbers, letters, colors, and objects are very prominent throughout the book. Point to each. This will help keep your audience members together as they shout their responses along with the kids in the book. There is also a little mouse that appears throughout the book. It will be hard to read his lines as the children shout, so once the book is finished, go back and share his lines.

- *Shhh!* A young boy tries very hard to be quiet while his baby brother naps. In his mind, his toys become life-size and he is very busy shushing them. He tells his clown to stop laughing, the tiger to stop growling, and the pirates to stop firing their cannons. When his brother wakes up, the clown can laugh again, the tiger can roar, and the pirates can fire their cannons.

  Storytelling Tips: The pictures show the boy holding his finger to his lips and saying "Shhh" to each of his toys. Cue the audience members to do the same. For instance, the boy tells his airplane pilot, "Please don't fly your buzzing plane." The kids in your audience can then put their fingers to their lips and say a quiet "Shhh."

Smile!

Final Lesson Plan

1. Opening Song: "Put on a Happy Face" by Maria Muldaur from *On the Sunny Side* (Music for Little People, 1990).
2. Picture Book: *Giggle, Giggle, Quack* by Doreen Cronin. Illustrated by Betsy Lewin. Simon & Schuster, 2002.
3. Poem: "I'm Glad I'm Me" by Jack Prelutsky from *My Dog May Be a Genius*. Illustrated by James Stevenson. Greewillow Books, 2008.
4. Picture Book: *Stuck* by Oliver Jeffers. Philomel Books, 2011.
5. Movement Activity: "Sticky, Sticky Bubblegum," traditional. Adapted by Rob Reid.
6. Picture Book: *Happy Belly, Happy Smile* by Rachel Isadora. Harcourt, 2009.
7. Musical Activity: "The Smiley Hokey Pokey," traditional. Adapted by Rob Reid.
8. Picture Book: *A Girl and Her Gator* by Sean Bryan. Illustrated by Tom Murphy. Arcade Publishing, 2006.
9. Nursery Rhyme/Movement Activity: "Hey, Diddle Diddle," traditional. Adapted by Rob Reid.
10. Picture Book: *Press Here* by Herve Tullet. Chronicle Books, 2011.

How I Got There

Initial Inspiration

It all started with my favorite book of the year: *Press Here*. I wanted to feature it in a program, but I had no idea what kind of theme to build around it. I didn't necessarily want to have a program with all toy and moveable books, the term assigned to *Press Here* by the Library of Congress. However, whenever I shared the book with little kids, their reaction was to smile (a possible theme), and to ask if it was magic (another possible theme). Since I had never conducted a "smile" theme before, the challenge was on.

The Scavenger Hunt

The terms "Smile," "Happy," "Happiness," and "Laughter" were plugged in for both word and subject searches. Only a handful of books came up, but luckily, there were some good ones. I added more search terms. We smile when someone takes our picture—a few more possibilities came up using the term "photography." The field grew substantially after adding silly stories to the hunt (after all, these kinds of books make us smile). I walked around the library and grabbed a few titles that had made me laugh in the past, and I even discovered a last-minute finalist sitting on the new book cart while making my rounds.

The Choices

- *A Girl and Her Gator* is one in a series that feature animals physically attached to children. The silliness of the concept won me over.
- *Giggle, Giggle, Quack* by Doreen Cronin is one of the sequels to *Click, Clack Moo: Cows that Type*. It's a silly story and the farm animals do a lot of smiling throughout the book.
- *Happy Belly, Happy Smile* by Rachel Isadora has a picture of a smiling boy on the cover. Inside the book, he finds happiness at his grandfather's restaurant.
- *Press Here* by Herve Tullet is the book I wanted to showcase in the first place.
- *Stuck* by Oliver Jeffers was the new book cart title. I smiled the whole time I read it.

Back-up Books Selection

- *Penguins* by Liz Pichon (Orchard Books, 2008) showcases several penguins who find a lost camera at the zoo. Of course, the penguins smile when they take pictures of each other.
- *Smile a Lot* by Nancy Carlson (Carolrhoda Books, 2002) features a frog with a huge smile on its face. How could anybody resist?
- *Ten Tiny Tickles* by Karen Katz (Simon & Schuster, 2005) showcases smiling family members gently tickling a smiling baby.

Choosing the Order of the Picture Books

Since *Press Here* was chosen as the "showcase book," should it be placed at the beginning of the program or at the end? I finally opted for the end because of the interactive, participative nature of the book. *Giggle, Giggle, Quack* and *Stuck* are the two longest books. *Stuck* was initially placed first, but after its accompanying activity was developed, it was moved to second in the line-up. *Happy Belly, Happy Smile* is a gentler book than the others, so it went in the middle for a nice, quiet moment. *A Girl and Her Gator* is the shortest book and got placed next-to-last, right before *Press Here*.

Locating and Creating the In-Between Activities

The "Smile" theme brought to mind two nursery rhymes. The first was "Mary Had a Little Lamb," with its line, "It made the children laugh and play to see a lamb at school." The second was "Hey, Diddle Diddle," with the line, "The little dog laughed to see such a sight." Was there a way to alter either one, or should they simply be read in the traditional way? I set those questions aside for the moment.

Several traditional songs were listed in *Children's Jukebox* under "Emotions-Happiness." Among those were the popular "The More We Get Together," and "If You're Happy and You Know It." They too, were set aside.

The picture book *Stuck* reminded me of the musical activity "Sticky Bubblegum" from the recording *Songs and Games for Toddlers* (Kids' Records, 1985) by Katherine Smithrim and Bob McGrath (Bob from Sesame Street). Inspired by that song, I wrote a little chant in which children could stick their hands on various things in the story program area. This new activity was paired with *Stuck* in the lesson plan order.

Next, I turned my attention back to the nursery rhymes. Perhaps "Hey, Diddle Diddle" could be recited along with the use of felt pieces. I was set to go that route when I wondered if we couldn't just act it out. From there, some motions and expressions were added. I put the finalized active piece near the end of the program.

Returning to the traditional songs, instead of "The More We Get Together" and "If You're Happy and You Know It," I chose to adapt another traditional song, "The Hokey Pokey." Rather than getting up and moving our bodies around, I thought it might work to make facial expressions. I practiced it in my office (I'm glad no one was around to see me), and then tried it on a few kids (my university office is close to the campus preschool). This made a good follow-up to *Happy Belly, Happy Smile*.

Program Presentation

Opening Song

"Put on a Happy Face" by Maria Muldaur from her recording *On the Sunny Side* (Music for Little People, 1990). As the children enter the program area, let them hear a recording of the modern-day classic "Put on a Happy Face." "Grey skies are going to clear up/ Put on a happy face." In addition to Muldaur's version, the song can also be found on the soundtrack of *Bye Bye Birdie* (RCA, 1963) and the children's recordings *Morning Magic* by Joanie Bartels (BMG, 1987).

Picture Book: *Giggle, Giggle, Quack*

Farmer Brown goes on vacation and leaves his brother Bob in charge of the animals. The duck begins to write instructional notes for Bob. "Tuesday night is pizza night (not the frozen kind!). The hens prefer anchovies." The animals are giggling as they watch Bob read the notes. Bob orders pizza. Duck continues to write orders on more notes. Bob follows them all, to the amusement of the animals.

Storytelling Tips: As set-up for the book, tell your audience that animals are going to trick a grown man. The animals giggle their way through the story and the kids should giggle, too. When they see the hens in the picture, they should giggle like hens. "Giggle, giggle, cluck." When they see pigs in the picture, they should "Giggle, giggle, oink," and so on.

Poem: "I'm Glad I'm Me"

This is a nice, short (eight-line) rhyming celebration of self. "There's no one else I want to be." It's one of Prelutsky's sweeter poems.

Picture Book: *Stuck*

A boy's kite gets stuck high in a tree. The boy throws his shoe at the kite but the shoe gets stuck, too. He throws his other shoe and "unbelievably, that got stuck as well." Next, the boy throws a cat up the tree. The cat gets stuck. The boy continues throwing things in the tree: a ladder, a bucket of paint, a duck, a kitchen sink, an orangutan, a small boat and a big boat, a blue whale, and much, much more. The boy finally knocks the kite down and leaves the tree. That night, in bed, the boy "could have sworn there was something he was forgetting."

Storytelling Tips: The absurdity of the objects the boy gathers and throws into the tree should be reflected in your voice and your facial expressions. Feel free to do "double-takes," looking at the picture, looking at the kids, and looking back and forth again rapidly.

Movement Activity: "Sticky, Sticky Bubblegum"

Recite this as a chant. Have the children clap their hands on "sticky, sticky bubblegum" before placing it on the object mentioned in the verse. Indicate that the last line, "stick it to the floor" means they should stick their bottoms to the floor and be ready to hear the next story.

Sticky, sticky bubblegum,
Sticky, sticky bubblegum,
Sticky, sticky bubblegum,
Stick it to your nose.

(Clap on all verses of "sticky, sticky bubblegum.")

(Put hands on your nose.)

Sticky, sticky bubblegum,
Sticky, sticky bubblegum,
Sticky, sticky bubblegum,
Stick it to your toes.

(Put hands on your toes.)

Sticky, sticky bubblegum,
Sticky, sticky bubblegum,
Sticky, sticky bubblegum,
Stick it to your peak.

(Place hands on top of head.)

Sticky, sticky bubblegum,
Sticky, sticky bubblegum,
Sticky, sticky bubblegum,
Stick it to your cheek.

(Place hands on cheeks.)

Sticky, sticky bubblegum,
Sticky, sticky bubblegum,
Sticky, sticky bubblegum,
Stick it to your seat.

(Put hands on your bottom.)

Sticky, sticky bubblegum,
Sticky, sticky bubblegum,
Sticky, sticky bubblegum,
Stick it to your feet.

(Put hands on your feet.)

Sticky, sticky bubblegum,
Sticky, sticky bubblegum,
Sticky, sticky bubblegum,
Stick it to the door.

(Walk over to the nearest door and place hands on it.)

Sticky, sticky bubblegum,
Sticky, sticky bubblegum,
Sticky, sticky bubblegum,
Stick it to the floor.

(Walk back to original sitting place and stick your bottom to the floor.)

Picture Book: *Happy Belly, Happy Smile*

Louie loves Fridays. That's when he visits his grandfather's Chinese restaurant. He goes back into the kitchen and says hello to the staff. It's very busy back there. Grandpa shouts that it's time to eat. Louie eats with chopsticks at the restaurant, "but most of the time at home I use a fork, knife, and spoon." Louie has a big smile on his face when he is served his favorite dish, "steamed dumplings, egg rolls, and shrimp chow mein." He doesn't smile at the fish and crabs, though. Louie opens his fortune cookie and Grandpa reads it. "Happy food, happy belly, happy smile."

Storytelling Tips: No need to do anything special while reading this nice, gentle, happy story. Afterwards, ask the kids what kind of food makes them smile.

Musical Activity: "The Smiley Hokey Pokey"

Instead of standing for the traditional versions of "The Hokey Pokey," this version can be done sitting down. Tell the children that sometimes you're happy, and sometimes you're sad and mad, too. It's normal to sometimes feel these emotions. Hopefully, most of the time, everyone will be happy.

You put your SMILE on,	*(Give a big smile.)*
You take your SMILE off,	*(Look blank.)*
You put your SMILE on,	*(Give a big smile.)*
And you shake it all around.	*(Move head around in a figure-eight motion while smiling.)*
You do the Hokey Pokey	*(Continue moving head.)*
And you show your great big SMILE,	*(Exaggerate smile.)*
That's what it's all about.	*(Clap twice.)*
You put your SAD FACE on,	*(Look sad. Perhaps stick lower lip out.)*
You take your SAD FACE off,	*(Look blank.)*
You put your SAD FACE on,	*(Look sad.)*
And you shake it all about.	*(Look at ground and shake head back and forth.)*
You do the Hokey Pokey	
And you show your poor SAD FACE,	*(Look sad.)*
That's what it's all about.	*(Clap twice.)*
You put your MAD FACE on,	*(Look mad.)*
You take your MAD FACE off,	*(Look blank.)*
You put your MAD FACE on,	*(Look mad.)*
And you shake it all about.	*(Cross arms and shake head back and forth.)*
You do the Hokey Pokey	
And you show your mean MAD FACE,	*(Look sad.)*
That's what it's all about.	*(Clap twice.)*

Pause and ask the kids if coming to Storytime makes them sad. Ask them if it makes them mad. Finally, ask them if coming to Storytime makes them happy and sing the "SMILE" verse one more time.

You put your SMILE on,	*(Give a big smile.)*
You take your SMILE off,	*(Look blank.)*
You put your SMILE on,	*(Give a big smile.)*
And you shake it all around.	*(Move head around in a figure-eight motion while smiling.)*
You do the Hokey Pokey	*(Continue moving head.)*
And you show your great big SMILE,	*(Exaggerate smile.)*
That's what it's all about.	*(Clap twice.)*

Picture Book: *A Girl and Her Gator*

A girl notices a gator on her head. The gator tells her, "Just let me hang out. These views are amazing and I love fresh air." The gator tells her all the things she could do with "a gator up there." She could "go to the fair with a gator up there" or give "her brother a scare with a gator up there." The girl sees the advantages but wonders what "should a girl wear with a gator up there?" This silly story is guaranteed to put smiles on the faces in your audience.

Storytelling Tips: The text is done in verse and flows quickly. Slow down when you get near the end. "What could be better? What else could compare?" Pause before turning to the final page where we see her cousin from Bel-Air "who woke up attached to a Kodiak Bear."

Nursery Rhyme/Movement Activity: "Hey, Diddle Diddle"

Ask the kids if they know the nursery rhyme, "Hey, Diddle Diddle." Ask them if they would laugh if they saw a cow jumping over the moon. Tell them you're going to recite it and that they should imitate the moves and sounds that you do. Note: you'll need to recite the rhyme slowly and put pauses in the middle of a few lines to make sure the kids can follow. Perform the piece one more time now that the children are a bit more familiar with the motions.

Hey, Diddle Diddle,	*(Twirl hands over each other.)*
The cat	*(Say "meow" right after "the cat.")*
and the fiddle,	*(Mime playing a violin.)*
The cow	*(Say "moo" right after "the cow" and put fingers on head for horns.)*
jumped over the moon.	*(I tried a variety of motions but got the biggest laugh when I said "Boing!" while lifting my hands.)*
The little dog	*(Say "woof" right after "the little dog.")*
laughed	*(Laugh.)*
to see such a sight.	*(Point and laugh again.)*
and the dish	*(Make a circle in the air with your finger.)*
ran away	*(Mime running by pumping your arms.)*
with the spoon.	*(Mime holding a spoon in your hands and then eating something with it.)*

Closing Picture Book: *Press Here*

Press a dot, turn the page, and another dot appears. Rub a dot, turn the page, and the dot changes color. Shake the book, turn the page, and the dots have moved. Blow on the page, turn the page, and the dots have moved again. Clap hands, turn the page, and the dots grow larger. This fun print version of an electronic game brings smiles on the kids' faces.

Storytelling Tips: If you have many children in the audience, perform the actions on the pages yourself, with the exception of the blowing air and clapping times. You can inform the kids that they can press the dots, themselves, after the program. If you have just a few children in the program, they can take turns pressing the dots for you.

Tips for Back-up Books

- *Smile a Lot!* While a frog goes through his day, he's reminded to keep smiling no matter what. "When Mom makes oatmeal with prunes for breakfast . . . Smile a lot! And ask if you can help her make chocolate chip pancakes tomorrow." The frog also learns that a smile helps when you're the new kid at school, facing tough guys, taking tests, going to the dentist, and practicing soccer. Finally, smile a lot when going to bed because "you've had a pretty good day!"

Storytelling Tips: Before you start reading, let the audience know that the phrase "smile a lot" comes up several times in the story. Each time it does, everyone should give a big smile.

- *Ten Tiny Tickles.* Adult family members tickle a baby all over her body in this counting board book. "One little tickle on a lovely, sleepy head." Baby wakes up when kitty tickles her two ears. She gets three tickles under her chin, four tickles on her hands while she's in the bathtub, and so on up to "ten tiny tickles on chubby, tubby toes." Baby is now ready for the day.

   Storytelling Tips: Have the audience members pretend-tickle themselves as the baby in the book gets her head, ears, chin, hands, tummy, arms, "tush," back, legs, and toes tickled.

- *Penguins.* After all of the zoo visitors have gone home, the penguins spot a camera in their exhibit. "What do you do with a camera?" asks one penguin. Another replies, "You smile at it!" The little penguin that found the camera tells the others to say, "FISH!" The penguins take turns taking pictures until the camera stops working. The next morning, the zookeeper takes the camera to the lost and found. The owner, a little girl, retrieves it. When the roll of film in her camera is developed, she is surprised to find up-close pictures of penguins.

   Storytelling Tips: There is a fold-out feature in the back of the book where the penguin photos can be viewed. Make a big deal out of unfolding the pictures. Afterwards, remind the children that the penguins said, "FISH!" when their picture was taken. What do we often say? "CHEESE!" What other animals might say "CHEESE?" Ask the children what other animals might say "FISH?"

Toyland, Toyland, Wonderful Girl and Boy Land

Final Lesson Plan

1. Opening Picture Book: *Hooray for Amanda and Her Alligator* (chapters 1, 2 & 2 ½) by Mo Willems. Balzer + Bray, 2011.
2. Movement Activity: "Teddy Bear, Teddy Bear," traditional.
3. Picture Book: *I Lost My Bear* by Jules Feiffer. HarperCollins, 1998.
4. Picture Book: *Hooray for Amanda and Her Alligator* (chapters 3 & 4).
5. Movement Activity: "Jack (and Jill) in the Box," traditional. New words by Rob Reid.
6. Picture Book: *My Bossy Dolly* by Steve Metzger. Scholastic, 2006.
7. Picture Book: H*ooray for Amanda and Her Alligator* (chapters 5 & 6).
8. Musical Activity: "The Eensy Weensy Robot," traditional. New words by Rob Reid.
9. Closing Picture Book: *Too Many Toys* by David Shannon. Scholastic, 2008.

How I Got There

Initial Inspiration

I had the song "Toyland" from the Disney movie, *Babes in Toyland,* stuck in my head, and this story program grew in part from that song. The original lyrics were tweaked just a bit for the title; the standard verse is "Toyland, toyland, little girl and boy land." The song and David Shannon's picture book, *Too Many Toys,* sparked the idea to develop a toy-themed lesson plan. Shannon's book contains exciting illustrations featuring dozens and dozens of toys that will delight young children.

The Scavenger Hunt

This search was easy and many quality hits were found within a short period of time. The terms "Toys," "Dolls," and "Teddy Bears" were used for subject and word searches. "Toys" yielded so many quality results that there was little need to depend too much on the other terms. Unsurprisingly, the search for "Teddy Bears" resulted in enough material to develop an entire lesson plan on teddy bears alone.

The Choices

- *Hooray for Amanda and Her Alligator* is made up of very short chapters within the picture book format. The potential is there to take the various chapters, each one a stand-alone story with a connecting plotline, and share them throughout the program.
- *I Lost My Bear* has wonderful, expressive dialogue.
- *My Bossy Dolly* can be read along with a real doll as a prop for an added visual element.
- *Too Many Toys* is very humorous and the illustrations will fascinate young children.

Back-up Books Selection

- *Chicken, Pig, Cow Horse Around* by Ruth Oni (Anic, 2011) is one book in a series that features toy animal protagonists.
- *The Trucker* by Barbara Samuels (Farrar, Straus and Giroux, 2010) will appeal to those many youngsters who love to play with toy trucks.
- *Where's My T-R-U-C-K?* by Karen Beaumont and illustrated by David Catrow (Dial, 2011)is a funny story about a boy searching for a lost toy truck. This title was moved to the Back-up Books Selection list because *I Lost My Bear* already featured a "my toy is missing" storyline.

Choosing the Order of the Picture Books

Amanda and her alligator are featured in "6 ½ Stories about 2 Surprising Friends." For this particular program, the chapters were divided into groups that are shared throughout the program. Since none of the remaining picture books chosen have a lot of audience participation elements in them, they were put in the order of longest to shortest. *I Lost My Bear* goes right after the first few chapters of *Amanda and Her Alligator*. *My Bossy Dolly* goes next in the lineup. Since there is a possibility of using a doll as a prop, this visual will work to hold the audience's attention during the middle of the program. *Too Many Toys*, with the shortest text and the most colorful illustrations, is the showcase piece and concludes the program.

Locating and Creating the In-Between Activities

"The Eensy Weensy Robot" was a fun adaptation to write. The idea came from perusing the usual roster of rhymes and songs. It was relatively easy to substitute the spider in "The Itsy Bitsy Spider" with a robot and then write two groups of four-line verses. This activity was paired with *Too Many Toys* because a toy robot can be found in the pictures.

"Teddy Bear, Teddy Bear" is a popular jump-rope/clapping chant that's been around for years. Many children may already know this fun activity. It has slower, gentler movements than the other activities and was placed near the beginning of the program.

There are a few versions of "Jack in the Box" on the Internet. Each version has children starting in a crouching position and springing upward like the old Jack-in-the-Box toy (if you have one, bring it in and demonstrate it to the kids). I tweaked the words to make a more suitable rhyme, and added "Jill" to the verse. This rambunctious activity was placed right before the mellow-but-funny *My Bossy Dolly*. Hopefully, the kids will be tired enough to settle down for it.

Program Presentation

Opening Picture Book: *Hooray for Amanda and Her Alligator* [**chapters 1, 2, and 2½**]

Read the first two chapters, plus chapter 2 ½, which is comprised of two sentences. These early chapters find Alligator waiting impatiently for Amanda to return from the library. When Amanda arrives, Alligator asks, "Do you have a surprise for me?" Amanda replies by shouting "Boo!" Alligator is scared but agrees that it was an interesting surprise. Later, Alligator tells Amanda he has a surprise for her. Amanda asks, "Is it you yelling Boo?" Alligator looks bummed out and says, "Not anymore." In chapter 2 ½, Alligator puts on his thinking cap and scares himself.

    Storytelling Tips: For these chapters and the other chapters to read later in the program, the dialogue will come easily because of Willems's approachable writing style. Be sure to point out the various library books that Amanda is reading, especially if there are any adults in the audience. The titles include *How to Raise a Tiger, Whale Songs for Beginners, Climbing Things for Fun and Profit,* and *You Can Make It Yourself: Jet Packs!*

Movement Activity: "Teddy Bear, Teddy Bear"

Have the children stand and act out the motions as you chant the lyrics.

Teddy Bear, Teddy Bear, turn around,	*(Turn in a circle.)*
Teddy Bear, Teddy Bear, touch the ground,	*(Bend over and touch the floor.)*
Teddy Bear, Teddy Bear, show your shoe,	*(Lift up on foot.)*
Teddy Bear, Teddy Bear, that will do.	*(Brush hands back and forth.)*
Teddy Bear, Teddy Bear, go upstairs,	*(March in place to mime climbing.)*
Teddy Bear, Teddy Bear, say your prayers,	*(Hold hands palm to palm.)*
Teddy Bear, Teddy Bear, switch off the light,	*(Mime flipping a light switch.)*
Teddy Bear, Teddy Bear, say "Good night!"	*(Wave.)*

Picture Book: *I Lost My Bear*

A little girl can't find her teddy bear and flies into over-the-top hysterics. Her sister gives her advice. "If you close your eyes and throw one of your other stuffed animals, sometimes it lands in the same place." The girl can't decide which one to throw next, so she picks one of her sister's stuffed animals. She eventually finds her bear under the covers of her very own bed.

    Storytelling Tips: The girl's mood is volatile, which make this book a fun read-aloud. One minute she's crying, the next she's reflective. Be extra dramatic with your vocal delivery when the girl climbs into bed and says, "I c-c-c-could-could-couldn't finnnnnnd her because yooo-ouuuuuuuu would-would-wouldn't hellllllllp meeeeeeeeee!"

Picture Book: *Hooray for Amanda and Her Alligator* [**chapters 3 and 4**]

Tell the kids it's time for more adventures featuring Amanda and her toy alligator. In these two chapters, Alligator is wearing his thinking cap. He tells Amanda that something tickles. When she asks, "What tickles?" Alligator springs at her and yells "I DO!" Later, Alligator is dismayed to find a price tag for seven cents on his tail. Amanda tells him he came from the "sale bucket." She cheers him up by telling him that no one else bought him "because they knew you were meant to be my best friend."

Movement Activity: "Jack (and Jill) in the Box"

Have the children stand and then chant the following:

Jack and Jill are in the box,   *(Crouch down.)*

When a kid opens the lid! POP!   *(Jump up.)*

Jack and Jill sink back again,   *(Slowly return to crouch position.)*

Until the kid opens the lid again! POP!   *(Jump up.)*

Repeat as many times as you'd like.

Picture Book: *My Bossy Dolly*

A young girl informs us that she's well behaved, but her dolly is not. When the girl tries to be quiet in the morning, her dolly yells, "Come on! Get up! Get out of bed! Give me milk to drink!" When her parents ask if that was her talking, the girl replies, "Oh no. That wasn't me. I'd never be a brat. It was my little dolly. Sometimes she talks like that." The dolly continues misbehaving and saying rude things. The girl concludes, "I'm glad I'm not that way!"

   Storytelling Tips: Hold up a doll in front of your face when the dolly has lines. This'll give the young audience members a clue that perhaps the little girl is making her doll act this way.

Picture Book: *Hooray for Amanda and Her Alligator* [chapters 5 & 6]

Alligator is bored and chews Amanda's head. She tells him to get a book. He chews the book. Alligator tells himself, "Books do beat boredom. But Amanda's head tastes better." In the last chapter, Alligator is surprised when Amanda returns from the zoo with a toy panda. "Alligator did not like Amanda's surprise." When Amanda leaves, the Panda grows impatient for her return. He convinces Alligator to join in singing and dressing up. Alligator decides that he has a new friend.

Musical Activity: "The Eensy Weensy Robot"

Have the children stand. Sing to the tune of "The Eensy Weensy Spider."

The Eensy Weensy Robot

Climbed to the table top.   *(Mime climbing with arms and feet.)*

Looked all around   *(Hand over eyes, look in all directions.)*

And gave a little hop.   *(Hop once.)*

Walked back and forth   *(Walk stiffly like a robot.)*

And looked so very brave.   *(Thump chest.)*

Then climbed into a spaceship   *(Mime climbing again.)*

And gave us one last wave.   *(Wave and then thrust arms in the air while making a "whoosh" noise.)*

Closing Picture Book: *Too Many Toys*

Spencer has so many toys that they "stretched from one corner of this house to the other and back again!" One day his mother yells, "YOU HAVE TOO MANY TOYS!" She orders Spencer to get rid of some. Of course, the boy protests, but he eventually selects several toys to give away and places them in a box. After a short rest, Spencer's mother returns to find that her son removed every toy from the box. "But we can't give away this box. It's the best toy EVER!"

   Storytelling Tips: The first half of the book shows how many toys Spencer owns and who gave them to him. Read this with a certain amount of awe in your voice as if you were an envious kid.

Tips for Back-up Books

- *Where's My T-R-U-C-K?* A young boy throws a fit over his missing truck. He looks all over the house (even disturbing someone in the shower). Everyone in the family tries to console him. He keeps saying, "I want my t-r-u-c-k!" His dog Bowser digs up the truck (and an odd assortment of other things that Bowser has apparently buried, including false teeth and an iPod).

  Storytelling Tips: Play up the boy's dialogue, especially when he spells out the word "truck." Let the kids linger over Catrow's wild illustrations. Someone may spot Bowser grabbing the buried items in his mouth early in the story.

- *Chicken, Pig, Cow Horse Around.* Chicken, Pig, and Cow are three toy friends. One day, a toy horse appears. Pig and Cow like him, but Chicken complains, "Horse takes up space." Chicken tricks Horse to play hide-and-seek, but doesn't tell the others. After Pig and Cow ask about Horse's whereabouts, Chicken feels guilty. The animals find Horse at the bottom of the fish bowl (or so Chicken thinks). Poor Chicken winds up inside the bowl. All of the other toys jump in to be with Chicken, and they work together to find a way out.

  Storytelling Tips: Read the book in a normal voice except for Chicken's lines. Give Chicken a slightly higher voice that has a snotty attitude at some times and a worried voice at other times.

- *The Trucker.* Leo loves playing with his toy trucks. "He said he could name a BILLION trucks." There are trucks everywhere in this house, even in his mother's oatmeal. His mother tries to open his world to things other than trucks. We see her reading the Travel section of the newspaper with the headline "10 Tropical Vacations." There is also a copy of the book, *How to Raise a Sensitive Boy* nearby. Mother brings home a cat. Leo is upset that the cat is not a new fire truck, but he soon incorporates the cat into his truck world.

  Storytelling Tips: When Leo plays with his fire truck, he yells, "WEE-OH" over and over. Say it once, then look at your audience and ask them if they will help make this noise with you.

Yawn: Stories and Activities about the End of the Day

Final Lesson Plan

1. Opening Picture Book: *Don't Let the Pigeon Stay Up Late!* by Mo Willems. Hyperion, 2006.
2. Movement Activity: "Yawn and Stretch" by Rob Reid, inspired by the nursery rhyme "The Grand Old Duke of York."
3. Picture Book: *Are You Awake?* by Sophie Blackall. Henry Holt & Company, 2011.
4. Picture Book: *Interrupting Chicken* by David Ezra Stein. Candlewick Press, 2010.
5. Musical Activity: "Good Night Children," traditional.
6. Picture Book/Felt Characters: *Whoo Goes There?* by Jennifer A. Ericsson. Illustrated by Bert Kitchen. Roaring Brook Press, 2009.
7. Musical Activity: "We Won't Go Home Until Morning," traditional.
8. Picture Book: *Tell Me the Day Backwards* by Albert Lamb. Illustrated by David McPhail. Candlewick Press, 2011.
9. Closing Activity/Memory Game: "Tell Me Your Day Backwards" inspired by the picture book, *Tell Me the Day Backwards*.

How I Got There

Initial Inspiration

The books *Interrupting Chicken* and *Tell Me the Day Backwards* were all the motivation I needed to do yet another bedtime story program. This is a popular theme for many libraries, and often, advertisements for bedtime-themed programs will invite audience members to attend wearing their pajamas. One fun bit of slapstick to do in a program like this is for the storyteller to yawn between picture books and then pretend to fall asleep. The kids, without fail, will giggle and yell, "Wake up!"

The Scavenger Hunt

It was easy to find titles searching with the terms, "Bedtime," "Night," and "Dreams"—the only problem was that the results were fairly overwhelming. I found it helpful to narrow the field by qualifying the search to list the hits by copyright date, newest to oldest. Since this theme has been popular for so long, and explored year after year over a long stretch, the newer titles refreshed the lesson planning.

The Choices

- *Are You Awake?* will especially appeal to any parent in the program who has had children wake them up by asking, "Are you awake?"
- *Don't Let the Pigeon Stay Up Late!* is one in a series of hilarious escapades starring a pigeon.
- *Interrupting Chicken* is a fun book to read in an "over-the-top" manner.
- *Tell Me the Day Backwards* is a feel-good story and a nice contrast to the many silly stories about bedtime.
- *Whoo Goes There?* is a good pattern story with felt character possibilities.

Back-up Books Selection

- *Good Night, World* by Willa Perlman and illustrated by Carolyn Fisher (Beach Lane Books, 2011) is an excellent opportunity to share phrases from around the world.
- *No Sleep for the Sheep!* by Karen Beaumont and illustrated by Jackie Urbanovic (Harcourt, 2011) has repetitive lines that can be taught to the audience.
- *Stop Snoring, Bernard!* by Zachariah OHora (Henry Holt & Company, 2011) also has potential for children to repeat lines from throughout the book.

Choosing the Order of the Picture Books

Tell Me the Day Backwards provides a unique opportunity to end the program with the quietest book. By placing this book at the end of the program, the children will have ample time to share their backwards-day stories. You can then end the entire program with the tag line, "I hope the next thing you do is check out library books." *Don't Let the Pigeon Stay Up Late!*, on the other hand, is a very active, very funny, short book. Use it to grab everyone's attention at the start of the program. *Are You Awake?* and *Interrupting Chicken* are good medium-length books. *Are You Awake?* has a quieter sense of humor and is a nice follow-up to the rambunctious pigeon book. *Interrupting Chicken* goes next because the dialogue can be delivered in a noisy manner. *Whoo Goes There?* may be accompanied by visuals in the form of felt characters, so place it next-to-last in the order.

Locating and Creating the In-Between Activities

Don't Let the Pigeon Stay Up Late! features a big yawn. I wanted to create an activity that encouraged the audience to yawn. Looking over the roster of rhymes and songs sparked the idea to use the nursery rhyme, "The Grand Old Duke of York." This traditional rhyme encourages children to stand and sit while the verses are read. Instead of standing and sitting, I altered it by replacing these movements with the raising and lowering of arms, as if stretching. The new version ends with a yawn.

For the next activity, the song "Goodnight Ladies" came to mind. It was easy to swap "ladies" with "children" for a quick and simple musical activity.

Finally, the song "We Won't Go Home until Morning" is presented as if nocturnal animals were singing the lyrics. This works well with *Whoo Goes There?*, a book about nocturnal animals. After turning the song into a circle marching activity, it made sense to place it near the end of the program.

Program Presentation

Opening Picture Book: *Don't Let the Pigeon Stay Up Late!*

The audience is to keep the pigeon from staying up late, but the pigeon does everything possible to avoid bedtime. The pigeon finally lets out a loud, "YAWN!" stating that it was just stretching, not yawning. The pigeon then falls asleep.

Storytelling Tips: After you read the loud "YAWN," don't be surprised to see some kids in the audience start yawning. Pigeon lets out a few more yawns before heading to dreamland. Point out that the Pigeon has a Knuffle Bunny, a toy from another Mo Willems series.

Movement Activity: "Yawn and Stretch"

(Inspired by the nursery rhyme, "The Grand Old Duke of York.")

You poor tired girls and boys,

You "yawn" the biggest yawn,	*(Yawn.)*
Your hands go way up high,	*(Stretch both arms overheard.)*
And back down with a sigh,	*(Lower arms and sigh.)*
And when they're up, they're up,	*(Stretch them overhead again.)*
And when they're down, they're down,	*(Lower arms.)*
And when you "yawn" again and again,	*(Yawn.)*
They're neither up	*(Point up with one finger.)*
Nor down.	*(Point down with the same finger.)*
'Cause they're covering your mouth!	*(Yawn and cover mouth with both hands. Say this last line as an aside.)*

Picture Book: *Are You Awake?*

A boy wakes up his mother. He asks her is she's awake. She tells him she's asleep because it's still nighttime. He asks, "Why is it still nighttime?" They continue their "discussion" with the mother patiently (and sleepily) responding to her son's stream of questions.

Storytelling Tips: This is a fun book to read aloud. Start out by reading the boy's lines in a loud whisper. "Mom? Mom?" Read the rest of his lines in a normal child's voice. Read the mother's lines as if you're half-asleep. Gradually, switch over to a patient, grown-up voice when it's apparent the child isn't going to fall asleep anytime soon.

Picture Book: *Interrupting Chicken*

Papa is reading stories to the little red chicken. He starts with "Hansel and Gretel." Just as the title characters are going inside the candy cottage, the little red chicken interrupts by shouting, "Don't go in! She's a witch!" Papa warns the little red chicken about interrupting while he's reading. He begins other stories but the little red chicken keeps interrupting. She does this during "Little Red Riding Hood" and "Chicken Little." When Papa runs out of stories, the little red chicken reads to him.

Storytelling Tips: This is another fun story for "over-the-top" vocalization. Read Papa's voice in a calm manner, and then become very excited with both your voice and gestures when the little red chicken interrupts.

Musical Activity: "Good Night, Children"

Sung to the tune of "Good Night, Ladies." Sing the song through once for the children. Then sing it a second time and encourage them to join you. On "merrily we roll along," have the children roll their hands around each other.

Good night, children,

Good night, children,

Good night, children,

It's time to go to bed.

Merrily we roll along, roll along, roll along,

Merrily we roll along, as off to bed we go.

Picture Book/Felt Story: *Whoo Goes There?*

Owl is hungry and watchful. He hears a "rustle, rustle" and wonders if it could be "a fat little mouse just right for my dinner?" It's not a mouse, it's a cat. "Owl did not want cat for his dinner. Owl notices several other nocturnal creatures: a skunk, rabbit, fox, bat, porcupine, and beaver. It's not until he finally spots a mouse does he fly into action. There's a crash, and we see the mouse, safe and sound, looking for his own dinner.

Storytelling Tips: Make felt characters of the nine animals from the patterns on pages 78–80 and display them as each appears in the story. Encourage the children to make the many sound effects found in the book as you read the text.

Musical Activity: "We Won't Go Home until Morning"

Sung to the tune of "For He's a Jolly Good Fellow." Ask the children to pick one of the animals from the previous picture book and to pretend they are that animal. Tell them that their animals have been up all night and are now coming home. The children can march in a circle while you sing this song.

We won't go home until morning,

We won't go home until morning,

We won't go home until morning,

Till daylight does appear.

Till daylight does appear,

Till daylight does appear,

We won't go home until morning,

Till daylight does appear.

Picture Book: *Tell Me the Day Backwards*

Timmy Bear and his mother play the memory game "Tell Me the Day Backwards." Timmy recalls brushing his teeth before climbing into bed. Before that, he watched the sunset with his mother. Earlier, they had a picnic with Papa Bear. The two go on to recount the entire day up to the point when they awoke after a long winter's sleep.

Storytelling Tips: Read the story in a nice relaxed style to bring the program to the final quiet activity.

Closing Activity/Memory Game: "Tell Me Your Day Backwards," inspired by *Tell Me the Day Backwards*

Ask the children what they did immediately before they came into the story program area. Some will talk about coming into the library. Others might be confused and tell you they woke up. (That's okay, just keep going.) Continue to the next step by saying, "What did you do today before you came to the library?" Let everyone respond. It might take a few minutes. Do this one or two more times. Don't worry about making it all the way to the time they got out of bed. Some kids tell you they brushed their teeth, put on their clothes, got into their cars, etc. When it's time to leave, tell everyone that you hope the NEXT thing they do will be to check out library books.

Tips for Back-up Books

- *No Sleep for the Sheep!* Poor sheep is awoken by a "Quack" at the door. Duck comes in and falls asleep next to sheep. Next, sheep wakes up because he hears a "Baaa" at the door. Goat comes in and joins the other two. There is a progression of animals that wake sheep with their respective noises. When they all finally fall asleep, rooster goes "Cock-a-Doodle-Doo" to announce daybreak. "But the sheep slept right on through . . ."

  Storytelling Tips: Once again, simple pattern stories are wonderful for story programs. The kids can learn the repetitive lines and vocally participate with the story. Sheep tells each of the other characters. "'Shhh! Not a peep! Get to sleep!'" Teach this phrase to the kids, right before you begin reading the book. Give them a visual cue, such as a nod of the head, when they should recite it.

- *Stop Snoring, Bernard!* Bernard is an otter that keeps the other animals in the zoo awake with his snoring. "One afternoon at naptime," another otter named Grumpy Giles tells Bernard to "snore somewhere else!" Bernard goes to the zoo lake, the fountain, a puddle, and a cave. Many animals yell "Stop snoring, Bernard!" The otters finally realize they miss Bernard and his snoring. They beg him to come back.

  Storytelling Tips: Have the audience say the lines, "Stop snoring, Bernard." Teach them to recite this line with a "scolding" wag of the finger.

- *Goodnight, World.* A child says goodnight to the sun, stars, planets, and all of the natural things on earth. "Good night, world, as darkness brings sweet dreams to every living thing."

  Storytelling Tips: The appendix contains many ways to say "good night" from around the world, Spanish, Mandarin, Vietnamese, Turkish, and other languages are represented. Share some examples with the kids. Ask the children to repeat them after you. A pronunciation guide is provided.

A Fun Example of a "Quick and Dirty" Program

When time is short, many storytellers grab a few picture books off the shelves, pull up a few in-between activities that they've used for years, and present a fairly successful story program with very little preparation. My staff used to call these programs "quick and dirty." While this happens to many of us, I feel it's best not to get into the habit too often. It will ultimately erode the quality of your story programs.

When the days do get away from you and you have just a few minutes of prep time, one fun approach to a hastily put-together program is to take a "What's Next?" approach. This idea was inspired by Laura Numeroff's picture book series that begins with *If You Give a Mouse a Cookie* (HarperCollins, 1985). Characters make imaginative leaps from one item or action to another. In the first book, if you give a mouse a cookie, he's going to want a glass of milk. The milk leads to a straw, the straw leads to a napkin, and so forth. With a "What's Next?" format, the storyteller can start with one picture book, select some aspect of the storyline or illustrations, and use that to make a connection to another picture book. A lot depends on the storyteller's knowledge of the picture book collection.

Here's an example:

Start with the picture book *Lola Loves Stories* by Anna McQuinn (Charlesbridge, 2010). Lola loves going to the library. She is inspired to dress up like storybook characters. The book ends with Lola dressed like Max from Maurice Sendak's *Where the Wild Things Are* (HarperCollins, 1963), a natural choice to include in the program. Since this second picture book features monsters, pick another monster book. Dav Pilkey's book, *The Hallo-weiner* (Scholastic, 1993), shows a dog chasing a "monster." Look for a dog book next. *If You Give a Dog a Donut* (Balzer + Bray, 2011) is another title in the Numeroff series. A donut is featured, so pick a food book to end the program. *Bear Wants More* by Karma Wilson (Margaret K. McElderry Books, 2003) is a story about a bear that is hungry and his friends help feed him. To sum up, the five picture books were chosen in a fun fashion for a "quick and dirty" program. Connections were made from storybook characters, to monsters, to dogs, to food.

Next, add some in-between activities to the program. You don't have a lot of time to create new activities, so go to your favorite core resources. The story program staple "Going on a Bear Hunt" can be paired with the Wilson bear book. This activity has been around for years, and it's still fun for storytellers and kids. I spent many years singing "Do Your Ears Hang Low?" while wearing tights on my head to resemble dog ears. This song can go between *The Hallo-weiner* and *If You Give a Dog a Donut*. Two activities down, one to go. A quick check of *Children's Jukebox* shows there are approximately 18 recorded songs about monsters under the heading, "Imaginary Characters/Creatures—Monsters." One of the songs is based on *Where the Wild Things Are*. This song, "I'm Wild," is an interactive song from the recording *Literacy in Motion* by the Learning Station (The Learning Station, 2005).

Call this program "What's Next?" and say this phrase to the audience in between each book. Here's the final lesson plan. Note that the order of the books and activities is selected based on the connections between books instead of the length of the texts.

1. Opening Picture Book: *Lola Loves Stories*
2. Picture Book: *Where the Wild Things Are*
3. Musical Activity: "I'm Wild"
4. Picture Book: *The Hallo-wiener*
5. Song: "Do Your Ears Hang Low"
6. Picture Book: *If You Give a Dog a Donut*
7. Picture Book: *Bear Wants More*
8. Closing Movement Activity: "Going on a Bear Hunt"

What if you wanted to go a different way with this program? Here's a different direction one can take going from the book *Lola Loves Stories*. Lola dresses up like storybook characters. Another literary character who dresses up as storybook characters is the title character from *Miss Brooks Loves Books (And I Don't)* by Barbara Bottner (Knopf, 2010). She loves books, so find a book about books. *Book! Book! Book!* by Deborah Bruss (A. Levine, 2001) features farm animals that want to read books. Pick a book about farms next. *Chickens to the Rescue* by John Himmelman (Henry Holt & Company, 2006) fits the bill. Now, just one more book is needed. Pick a book based on the concept of "rescue." Firefighters rescue people. *Firefighter Ted* by Andrea Beaty (Margaret K. McElderry Books, 2009) is a good title to wrap up the program. Again, check your core resources for appropriate in-between activities, and you have completely different "quick and dirty" programs.

Part 3
Rob's Favorites

A Collection of Original and Adapted Fingerplays, Songs, and Other In-Between Activities

"A Book! Bok! Bok!" (Chant)

Repeat each verse twice. Have the audience join you the second time. Eventually, the children will chime in with the name of the animal based on the sound cue before you say it.

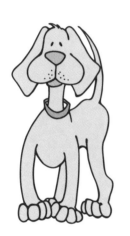

A book! Bok! Bok!
A book! Bok! Bok!
A chicken's got a book! Bok! Bok!

A book! Bow Wow!
A book! Bow Wow!
A dog has got a book! Bow Wow!

A book! Baa! Baa!
A book! Baa! Baa!
A sheep has got a book! Baa Baa!

A book! Buzz! Buzz!
A book! Buzz! Buzz!
A bee has got a book! Buzz! Buzz!

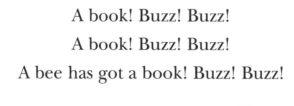

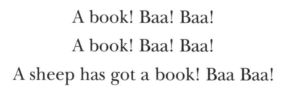

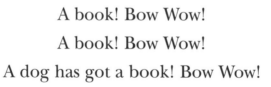

"The Bundle-Up Dance" (Musical Activity)

Sung to the tune of "Baby Shark."

Bundle-up, doot-doot-doodley-doot,
Bundle-up, doot-doot-doodley-doot.

Snow pants, doot-doot-doodley-doot, *(Mime putting on snow pants.)*
Snow pants, doot-doot-doodley-doot.

Winter coat, doot-doot-doodley-doot, *(Mime putting on winter coat.)*
Winter coat, doot-doot-doodley-doot.

Two boots, doot-doot-doodley-doot, *(Mime putting on boots.)*
Two boots, doot-doot-doodley-doot.

Warm hat, doot-doot-doodley-doot, *(Mime putting on hat.)*
Warm hat, doot-doot-doodley-doot.

Long scarf, doot-doot-doodley-doot, *(Mime wrapping scarf around neck.)*
Long scarf, doot-doot-doodley-doot.

Two gloves, doot-doot-doodley-doot, *(Mime putting on gloves.)*
Two gloves, doot-doot-doodley-doot.

Let's play, doot-doot-doodley-doot, *(Dance in place.)*
In the snow, doot-doot-doodley-doot.

Bundle-up! Yeah!

"Dogs and Cats and Guinea Pigs" (Musical Activity)

Sung to the tune of "Head, Shoulders, Knees and Toes."
When singing these words, perform the following motions:

Dogs: Pant with tongues out.

Cats: Pretend to lick hands as if they are paws.

Guinea Pigs: Blink as if just waking up and looking around.

Birds: Flap arms as wings.

Fish: Purse lips and hold hands behind ears as if they were gills.

Snakes: Flick tongues in and out.

Mice: Brush behind ears as if cleaning them with paws.

Dogs and cats and guinea pigs,

Guinea pigs.

Dogs and cats and guinea pigs,

Guinea pigs.

Birds and fish and snakes and mice,

Dogs and cats and guinea pigs,

Guinea pigs.

"Goldilocks" (Musical Activity)

Sung to the tune of "Over in the Meadow."

Goldilocks went to the home of the bears,

She decided to sample their wares,

She ate their porridge and then she cried,

'It's too hot!' (Make an expression as if you ate something hot while fanning mouth)

'It's too cold!' (Scrunch face, hug self, and shake whole body as if shivering)

And then, 'It's just right!' (Make a circle with thumb and pointer finger and wink)

Goldilocks went to the home of the bears,

She decided to sample their wares,

She sat on their chairs and then she cried,

'It's too hard!' (Rub bottom as if it is sore)

'It's too soft!' (Hold arms overhead and wiggle downward as if sinking)

And then, 'It's just right!' (Make a circle with thumb and pointer finger and wink)

Goldilocks went to the home of the bears,

She decided to sample their wares,

She crawled into their beds and then she cried,

'It's too hard!' (Hold body stiff as a board with arms alongside)

'It's too soft!' (Repeat the motions you did for the soft chair)

And then, 'It's just right!' (Pretend to fall asleep)

Goldilocks slept in the home of the bears,

She didn't hear them climbing up the stairs,

They woke her up and then she cried, (Pause)

"AAAAAAAAAAHHHHHHHH!!!!!" (Have everyone scream)

"The Happy, Sad, Mad Nursery Rhyme" (Choral Reading)

Have the kids pick a nursery rhyme and recite it three times. The first time, recite it with a happy voice. The second time, recite it with a sad voice. Recite it the third time with a mad voice. The end result is usually laughter. My groups have had particular fun with "Jack and Jill," "Hickory Dickory Dock," and "Little Miss Muffet."

"Hey You, Hey Me!" (Chant)

Chant this little ditty or sing any notes that come to mind. Have the kids repeat after you.

Hey you!

Hey me!

Look'ee here!

I'm a tree!
(Have everyone stand and display their branches.)

2 . . . I'm a bee . . .
(Make flying motions and buzzing noises.)

3 . . . I'm a chimpanzee . . .
(Make ape noises and movements.)

4 . . . We are WE! . . .
(Point to each other or do a group hug.)

"If You're a Ghost and You Know It" (Musical Activity)

Sung to the tune of "If You're Happy and You Know It."

If you're a ghost and you know it, say "Boo!" (Boo!)

If you're a ghost and you know it, say "Boo!" (Boo!)

If you're a ghost and you know, then your face will surely show it,

If you're a ghost and you know it, say "Boo!" (Boo!)

2. Black cat . . . say "Meow!" (Meow!)

3. Bat . . . flap your wings. (Flap)

4. Skeleton . . . rattle your bones. (Wiggle)

"If You're Worried and You Know It" (Musical Activity)

Sung to the tune of "If You're Happy and You Know It."

If you're worried and you know it, hug yourself.

If you're worried and you know it, hug yourself.

If you're worried and you know it,
Then your face will surely show it.

If you're worried and you know it, hug yourself.

2. If you're sad and you know it, cry "Boo-hoo."

3. If you're blue and you know it, dance away!

4. If you're happy and you know it, clap and dance.

"I'm Mad! Stomp! Stomp!" (Movement Activity)

This is a call-and-response activity. Stomp your feet and chant. Ask the audience to take a turn and imitate you.

I'm mad! Stomp! Stomp!

I'm mad! Stomp! Stomp!

I'm mad! I'm mad! I'm mad!

Stomp! Stomp!

I'm mad! Hop! Hop!

I'm mad! Hop! Hop!

I'm mad! I'm mad! I'm mad!

Hop! Hop!

I'm mad! Scream! Scream!

I'm mad! Scream! Scream!

I'm mad! I'm mad! I'm mad!

Scream! Scream!

(Pause.)

I'm taking control.

I'm going to Freeze!

(Stand motionless for a few seconds.)

Whew. *(Wipe brow.)*

I feel much, much better.

"The More We Brush Our Teeth" (Musical Activity)

Sung to the tune of
"The More We Get Together."

The more we brush our teeth,

(Mime brushing.)

Our teeth, our teeth,

The more we brush our teeth,

The healthier we'll be.

Brush this way and that way,

And that way and this way,

The more we brush our teeth,

The healthier we'll be.

The more we floss our teeth,

(Mime flossing.)

Our teeth, our teeth,

The more we floss our teeth,

The healthier we'll be.

Floss this way and that way,

And that way and this way,

The more we floss our teeth,

The healthier we'll be.

"My Face" (Chant)

Have the kids make appropriate faces as you share this little chant.

My oh my, my oh my, I've got my mad face on!

My oh my, my oh my, I've got my sad face on!

My oh my, my oh my, I've got my surprised face on!

My oh my, my oh my, I've got my worried face on!

My oh my, my oh my, I've got my happy face on!

Follow up by going through the facial expressions as a drill: Mad! Sad! Happy! Worried! Surprised! Mad! Happy! Sad!

"Old MacDonald Had a Jungle" (Musical Activity)

Sung to the tune of "Old MacDonald."

Old MacDonald had a jungle, E-I-E-I-O.

And in that jungle he had a monkey, E-I-E-I-O.

With a Ooh-Ooh here and a Ooh-Ooh there,

Here an Ooh, there an Ooh,

Everywhere an Ooh-Ooh,

Old MacDonald had a jungle, E-I-E-I-O.

2. Elephant . . . With a (trumpet noise) here and a (trumpet noise) there,

3. Lion . . . With a ROAR-R-R here and a ROAR-R-R there,

4. Snake . . . With a Hiss-Hiss here and a Hiss-Hiss there,

5. Hyena . . . With a Hee-Hee here and a Ha-Ha there,

"Old MacDonald Had an Owl" (Musical Activity)

Sung to the tune of "Old MacDonald."

Old MacDonald had a farm, E-I-E-I-O.

And on this farm he had an Owl! E-I-E-I-O.

With a "Whoo Whoo" here, (Flap arms.)

And a "Whoo Whoo" there,

Here a "Whoo," there a "Whoo,"

Everywhere a "Whoo Whoo."

Old MacDonald had a farm, E-I-E-I-O.

2. Ogre . . . With an "Aargh Aargh" here and an "Aargh Aarg" there . . . *(Shake fists.)*

3. Octopus . . . With a "Hug Hug" here and a "Hug Hug" there . . .
(Wrap arms around your body.)

4. Onion . . . With a "Waah Waah" here and a "Waah Waah" there . . .
(Fists on eyes as if crying.)

"Penguin Goes Shopping for Clothes." (Felt Story)

Make a felt penguin and multi-colored "tuxedos." Place them on the felt board at the appropriate times. Instruct the kids ahead of time to tell the penguin "NO!" when the penguin asks their opinion.

A penguin walked into a clothing store. *(Place penguin on board.)*

He said, "I'm tired of wearing black and white all of the time. Do you have anything colorful I can wear?"

"We sure do," said the storekeeper. "We have a new line of colorful tuxedos. Let's try on this red one." *(Place the red tux on the penguin.)*

"Hmm, not bad," said the penguin. "Hey, you kids. Do you think I look good in red?"

(Kids respond "NO!")

"Let me try on another outfit," said the penguin to the storekeeper.

The storekeeper said, "Let's try on this yellow one."

"Hmm, not bad," said the penguin. "Hey, you kids. Do you think I look good in yellow?"

(The kids respond "NO!" Repeat this pattern with other colors. Consider making checks, plaids, stripes, etc.)

The storekeeper finally said, "That's the last one."

The penguin thought a moment. "Maybe I should have asked those kids if I looked good in black and white. Hey, you kids. Do you think I look good in black and white?"

(If the kids respond mostly "YES," then place the black tux back on the penguin and have the penguin thank the kids. If the kids respond mostly with "NO," then have the penguin say, "Guess I'll go with just white.")

"The Penguins All March in a Line" (Musical Activity)

Sung to the tune of "The Ants Go Marching." Have everyone stand up and march with their arms at their sides like a penguin. They can wave their "flippers" on the appropriate line.

The penguins all march in a line,

Hurrah, hurrah.

The penguins all march in a line,

Hurrah, hurrah.

The penguins all march in a line,

They wave their flippers at the same time.

Yes, the penguins all march in a line, a very straight line.

"The Raccoon's Hunt" (Movement Activity)

This activity is based on the traditional activity "Going on a Bear Hunt."

We're going on a hunt for food. *(We're going on a hunt for food.)*

We're creeping past a human's house. *(We're creeping past a human's house.)*

Shh! *(Shh!)*

We need to be quiet. *(We need to be quiet.)*

What's that? *(What's that?)*

Bark! Bark! Bark! Bark! *(Bark! Bark! Bark! Bark!)*

A dog! *(A dog!)*

Run away! *(Run away!)*

Whew, that was close. *(Whew, that was close.)*

Let's try again. *(Let's try again.)*

We're going on a hunt for food. *(We're going on a hunt for food.)*

We're creeping past a human's house. *(We're creeping past a human's house.)*

Shh! *(Shh!)*

We need to be quiet. *(We need to be quiet.)*

What's that? *(What's that?)*

Honk! Honk! *(Honk! Honk!)*

A car! *(A car!)*

Run away! *(Run away!)*

Whew, that was close. *(Whew, that was close.)*

Let's try again. *(Let's try again.)*

We're going on a hunt for food. *(We're going on a hunt for food.)*

We're creeping past a human's house. *(We're creeping past a human's house.)*

Shh! *(Shh!)*

We need to be quiet. *(We need to be quiet.)*

What's that? *(What's that?)*

Hey, it's a trash can! *(Hey, it's a trash can!)*

Oops! We knocked it over! *(Oops! We knocked it over!)*

Crash! Crash! Rattle! Bang! *(Crash! Crash! Rattle! Bang!)*

Oh well. *(Oh well.)*

Let's eat! *(Let's eat!)*

Please pass the fish heads. *(Please pass the fish heads.)*

Yum! Yum! *(Yum! Yum!)*

"R-O-B-O-T" (Musical Activity)

Sung to the tune of "B-I-N-G-O"

There was a brilliant genius kid,
He built a real cool robot.
R-O-B-O-T, R-O-B-O-T, R-O-B-O-T,
He built a real cool robot.

(For each subsequent verse, remove a letter from the word "Robot," and
substitute it with a clap of the hands and a verbal "Clank!")

There was a brilliant genius kid,
He built a real cool robot.

[Clank]-O-B-O-T, [Clank]-O-B-O-T, [Clank]-O-B-O-T,
He built a real cool robot.

There was a brilliant genius kid,
He built a real cool robot.
[Clank]-[Clank]-B-O-T, [Clank]-[Clank]-B-O-T, [Clank]-[Clank]-B-O-T,
He built a real cool robot.

There was a brilliant genius kid,
He built a real cool robot.
[Clank]-[Clank]-[Clank]-O-T, [Clank]-[Clank]-[Clank]-O-T,
[Clank]-[Clank]-[Clank]-O-T,
He built a real cool robot.

There was a brilliant genius kid,
He built a real cool robot.
[Clank]-[Clank]-[Clank]-[Clank]-T, [Clank]-[Clank]-[Clank]-[Clank]-T,
[Clank]-[Clank]-[Clank]-[Clank]-T,
He built a real cool robot.

There was a brilliant genius kid,
He built a real cool robot.
[Clank]-[Clank]-[Clank]-[Clank]-[Clank], [Clank]-[Clank]-
[Clank]-[Clank]-[Clank], [Clank]-[Clank]-[Clank]-[Clank]-[Clank],
He built a real cool robot.

She'll be driving a bulldozer

When she comes.

Push it back! *(Hold hands palm out and move them away from body.)*

She'll be driving a bulldozer

When she comes.

Push it back!

She'll be driving a bulldozer,

She'll be driving a bulldozer,

She'll be driving a bulldozer

When she comes.

Push it back!

2. She'll be running a big digger when she comes. Scoop it up!
(Make a scooping motion with hands.)

3. She'll be working a dirt-dumper when she comes. Look out below!
(Cup hand around mouth.)

4. She'll be on a cement mixer when she comes. Shake it up! *(Shake your body.)*

5. She'll be steering a steamroller when she comes. Roll it flat! *(Twirl arms around each other.)*

6. She'll be driving a street sweeper when she comes. Clean it up!
(Make sweeping motions with hands.)

"Stamp Your Feet" (Movement Activity)

Instruct the kids to stand and act out the motions while you chant the words.
This is a good "shake your wiggles out" activity.

Stamp your feet, clap your hands.
Stamp your feet, clap your hands.
Stamp your feet, clap your hands.
Stamp your feet, clap your hands.

Nod your head, wiggle your bum.
Nod your head, wiggle your bum.
Nod your head, wiggle your bum.
Nod your head, wiggle your bum.

Stamp your feet, clap your hands.
Stamp your feet, clap your hands.
Stamp your feet, clap your hands.
Stamp your feet, and sit back down.

"The Teeny-Tiny Kid" (Movement Activity)

Have everyone stand. Emphasize "teeny" with your voice.

When I was a teeny-teeny-teeny tiny kid

I was just this big!

(Indicate a two-inch space between thumb and pointer finger.)

When I was a teeny-teeny tiny kid

I was just this big! *(Hold hand flat by knees.)*

When I was a teeny tiny kid

I was just this big! *(Hold hand flat by waist.)*

When I was a tiny kid

I was just this big! *(Hold hand flat by nose.)*

Some kids want to be this big!

(Stand on tiptoes and stretch arms high overhead.)

But I'm the

Right-sized kid! *(Hold hand on top of head.)*

There's a Monster Behind Me! (Fingerplay)

Place one hand behind you and wiggle all five fingers. Close your eyes while reciting the fingerplay rhyme.

There's a monster behind me, behind me, oh golly gee!

There's a monster behind me, oh golly gee!

(Move your hand with the wiggling fingers next to one of your ears.)

Now the monster's on my ear, on my ear, oh dear!

Now the monster's on my ear, oh dear!

(Move your hand with the wiggling fingers to the top of your head.)

Now the monster's in my hair, in my hair, beware!

Now the monster's in my hair, beware!

(Move your hand with the wiggling fingers in front of your face.)

Now the monster's by my eye, by my eye, oh my!

Now the monster's by my eye, oh my!

(Slowly open your eyes while making whimpering sounds. Look surprised and then happy at finding only wiggling fingers instead of a monster.)

Hey, that's no monster!

Golly gee! Oh dear! Beware? Oh my!

"Three Little Aliens" (Fingerplay)

Make a flying saucer with your left hand by making a fist. Hold up three fingers with your right hand and place this hand on top of the left hand. It should resemble three aliens in a flying saucer. Move both hands around while you recite the fingerplay as if the flying saucer was traveling through space.

Three little aliens,

Throughout outer space they flew,

One landed on Jupiter, *(Hold up one finger on right hand and move it far from the left hand.)*

And then there were two. *(Hold up two fingers over the "flying saucer.")*

Two little aliens,

Circled 'round the sun,

One got a bit too close, *(Hold up one finger on right hand and move it far from the left hand.)*

And now there is one. *(Hold up one finger over the "flying saucer.")*

One little alien,

Did not want to be a zero,

We now call him Superman,

Our very own super-hero! *(Make muscles with both arms.)*

Follow up this fingerplay by telling the kids that the imaginary character Superman came from the pretend planet Krypton, thus making him an alien. He landed on Earth and became one of our most popular comic super-heroes.

"Trip Trap, Trip Trap, Who's That?" (Guessing Game Activity)

Think of various bad guys and gals in children's literature and share simple, one-line descriptions of them to your young audience. To start this activity, have the kids pretend they live under a bridge. Have them slap their legs like they did for the previous picture book and say, "Trip trap, trip trap, who's that?" Have them repeat these actions and lines between each of the leader's character descriptions. After the leader's lines, the kids can then make their guesses.

Kids: "Trip trap, trip trap, who's that?"

Leader: I have sharp teeth and I love bats. (A vampire/Dracula)

Kids: "Trip trap, trip trap, who's that?"

Leader: I have sharp teeth and howl at the moon. (Wolves/the big, bad wolf/werewolves)

Kids: "Trip trap, trip trap, who's that?"

Leader: I like to fly on a broom. (A witch)

Kids: "Trip trap, trip trap, who's that?"

Leader: I live at the top of a beanstalk. (A giant)

Kids: "Trip trap, trip trap, who's that?"

Leader: I like to say "Boo!" (A ghost)

The Twelve Days of Storytime (Musical Activity)
Sung to the tune "The Twelve Days of Christmas."

On the first day of Storytime,
The 'teller shared with me,
A book about a curious monkey.

On the second day of Storytime,
The 'teller shared with me,
Two Dr. Seuss,
And a book about a curious monkey.

On the third day of Storytime,
The 'teller shared with me,
Three fingerplays,
Two Dr. Seuss,
And a book about a curious monkey.

On the fourth day of Storytime,
The 'teller shared with me,
Four funny poems,
Three fingerplays,
Two Dr. Seuss,
And a book about a curious monkey.

On the fifth day of Storytime,
The 'teller shared with me,
Five animal noises, (Invite the audience
members to make animal noises every
time you reach this part of the verse.)
Four funny poems,
Three fingerplays,
Two Dr. Seuss,
And a book about a curious monkey.

On the sixth day of Storytime,
The 'teller shared with me,
Six arts and crafts,
Five animal noises,
Four funny poems
Three fingerplays,
Two Dr. Seuss,
And a book about a curious monkey.

On the seventh day of Storytime,
The 'teller shared with me,
Seven pop-up books,
Six arts and crafts,
Five animal noises,
Four funny poems,
Three fingerplays,
Two Dr. Seuss,
And a book about a curious monkey.

On the eighth day of Storytime,
The 'teller shared with me,
Eight sing-along songs,
Seven pop-up books,
Six arts and crafts,
Five animal noises,
Four funny poems,
Three fingerplays,
Two Dr. Seuss,
And a book about a curious monkey.

On the ninth day of Storytime,
The 'teller shared with me,
Nine nursery rhymes,
Eight sing-along songs,
Seven pop-up books,
Six arts and crafts,
Five animal noises,
Four funny poems,
Three fingerplays,
Two Dr. Seuss,
And a book about a curious monkey.

On the tenth day of Storytime,
The 'teller shared with me,
Ten Hokey-Pokeys,
Nine nursery rhymes,
Eight sing-along songs,
Seven pop-up books,
Six arts and crafts,
Five animal noises,
Four funny poems,
Three fingerplays,
Two Dr. Seuss,
And a book about a curious monkey.

On the eleventh day of Storytime
The 'teller shared with me,
Eleven puppet shows,
Ten Hokey-Pokeys,
Nine nursery rhymes,
Eight sing-along songs,
Seven pop-up books,
Six arts and crafts,
Five animal noises,
Four funny poems,
Three fingerplays,
Two Dr. Seuss,
And a book about a curious monkey.

On the twelfth day of Storytime,
The 'teller shared with me,
Twelve yummy treats,
Eleven puppet shows,
Ten Hokey-Pokeys,
Nine nursery rhymes,
Eight sing-along songs,
Seven pop-up books,
Six arts and crafts,
Five animal noises,
Four funny poems,
Three fingerplays,
Two Dr. Seuss,
And a book about a curious monkey.

"Wave Goodbye" (Movement Activity)

Wave high, *(Wave hand over head.)*

Wave low, *(Wave hand near the ground.)*

I think it's time *(Point to wrist as if wearing a watch.)*

We gotta go. *(Point to the door.)*

Wave your elbows, *(Wave elbows.)*

Wave your toes, *(Wave toes/feet)*

Wave your tongue, *(Stick out tongue and wave it.)*

And wave your nose. *(Wiggle nose.)*

Wave your knees, *(Wave knees.)*

Wave your lips, *(Move mouth all around.)*

Blow a kiss

With fingertips. *(Blow a kiss.)*

Wave your ears, *(Wiggle ears.)*

Wave your hair, *(Shake head.)*

Wave your belly, *(Shake belly.)*

And derriere. *(Shake rear end.)*

Wave your chin, *(Wiggle chin.)*

Wave your eye, *(Blink.)*

Wave your hand, *(Lift up hand.)*

And wave goodbye. *(Wave.)*

"We're Going on a Duck Hunt" (Movement Activity)

This activity is based on the traditional activity "Going on a Bear Hunt."

Chorus:

We're going on a duck hunt.

We're looking for a big duck.

We have our wings and our waddle.

We hope we have lots of good luck.

Look! A hill! *(Point.)*

Can't go over it.

Can't go under it. *(Make over and under motions with your hands.)*

We'll have to fly around it.

Flap, flap, flap, flap, flap. *(Make flapping motions while circling.)*

We did it!

(Repeat chorus.)

Look! A town! *(Point.)*

Can't go over it.

Can't go under it. *(Make over and under motions with your hands.)*

We'll have to waddle through it.

Waddle, waddle, waddle, waddle, waddle.

(Tuck arms in armpits and waddle in small circles.)

(Repeat chorus.)

Look! A pond! *(Point.)*

Can't go over it.

Can't go under it. *(Make over and under motions with your hands.)*

We'll have to swim on it.

Swim, swim, swim, swim, swim. *(With arms tucked in as wings,*
mime swimming by wiggling bottoms.)

Let's do a duck call.

Quack, quack, quack, quack, quack, quack, quack, quack, quack, quack!

Wait! What's that in the middle of the pond?

It's a duck!

Quack, quack, quack, quack, quack, quack, quack, quack, quack, quack!

Swim away! Swim, swim, swim, swim, swim!

Waddle away! Waddle, waddle, waddle, waddle, waddle!

Fly away! Fly, fly, fly, fly, fly!

Whew, that was close.

What's that?

Ducks aren't scary?

We should go back and make friends with the duck?

Okay, we'll do it all over again—tomorrow!

Quiet in the Garden Patterns

Enlarge as needed.

Quiet in the Garden Patterns

Enlarge as needed.

Quiet in the Garden Patterns

Enlarge as needed.

Quiet in the Garden Patterns

Enlarge as needed.

Whoo Goes There? Patterns

Enlarge as needed.

Whoo Goes There? Patterns

Enlarge as needed.

Whoo Goes There? Patterns

Enlarge as needed.